GW00480814

ISBN: 9798676162672

Imprint/Publisher: CreateSpace

Table of Contents

Unsolved 1988

- Rodney Lockwood
- Brian Hayward
- Louise Kay
- Marie Wilkes
- Noel Smith
- Brian Kerr
- Jason Clear
- Alicia Lamothe
- Joan Macan
- John Lewis
- Abdur Rashid
- Carol Baldwin
- Debbie Linsley
- Severed Limbs
- Michel Becouarn
- John Lennon
- John Lawrence
- Graeme Stack
- Ian Bushell
- Yana Jones
- Anthony Gardner

Unsolved 1988

A list of unsolved cases for 1988.

Man

Age: 28

Sex: male

Date: 19 Dec 1988

Place: City Lights Discotheque, Johnstone, Scotland

A man was stabbed in the City Lights Discotheque in Johnstone.

He was stabbed around midnight and died later in hospital.

Nothing more is known.

Peter Henry Hurburgh

Age: 57

Sex: male

Date: 15 Dec 1988

Place: Black Mans Lane, Chelsham, Surrey

Peter Henry Hurburgh was murdered on 15 December 1988. Three men were convicted of his murder at the Old Bailey on Monday 26 February 1990, but their convictions were later overturned on 17July 2000 following an appeal which ruled that because one of the witnesses was a police informant and had been paid for his evidence, a fact that was not disclosed at the time of the trial, that the case against them was as a result not safe. However, the judge noted that the appeal decision was based on a technicality and that the case against some of the men was still overwhelming and they were freed without a judicial declaration of innocence.

The 1990 trial had lasted six weeks, and the jury took five hours to reach its verdict. At the trial, the men, along with another accomplice, were described as 'acid house party freaks' who were 'driven by ecstasy and cocaine and the kill thrill'. It was said that they were not interested in the financial gain but were only in it for the kicks. A police spokesman said, 'The 1970s film 'A Clockwork Orange' is now a horrifying reality'.

Peter Hurburgh had been having sex with another man in his Austin Princess car which he had parked up in a field in Black Man's Lane in Chelsham in the early hours of Friday 16 December 1988, when they were attacked and tied up. Peter Hurburgh was beaten and died from heart failure. He also had five fractured ribs and a fractured sternum. His injuries had bruised his heart and had caused him to suffer from a cardiac arrest from which he died. His body was later found tied up hand and foot in a field.

Following Peter Hurburgh's death, the police said that they were linking his murder to a series of crimes committed by a group they were labelling as the M25 Gang and the M25 Three. It was later heard that the M25 Gang were based in Lawrie Park Road,

Sydenham but used the M25 to get to their targets and to return quickly. Two other robberies were committed on the same night that were connected with the gang as well as a number of other crimes on previous dates.

It was said that the three men convicted of his murder, aged 21, 23 and 25 had gone out in a stolen Triumph Spitfire car on the night of 16 December 1988 and that when they came across Peter Hurburgh and his friend that they had attacked them, armed with a gun and a machete.

They poured petrol over the two men and beat Peter Hurburgh about the head and chest and kicked him, and it was said that after pouring the petrol over them that one of them had lit a cigarette. They then stole £10 from the man that Peter Hurburgh was with and drove off with his Austin Princess car. Peter Hurburgh's friend said that when the gang arrived, they were dragged from their car and stripped and beaten and that he soon after lost consciousness and that when he woke up he found Peter Hurburgh tied up and dead.

At the trial, the 20-year-old friend said that they had been dragged from the car and trussed up like chickens with rope and gagged. He said, 'While I was being searched, I could hear shouting and screaming coming from the car. I got the impression that Peter was being dragged from the car. I couldn't see properly because I was face down'.

In the initial stages of the investigation the police said that it was possible that one of the attackers might have been injured in the attack on Peter Hurburgh and his friend, stating that it was possible that he had turned a machete on his killers.

It was said that following the attack that the gang drove off in Peter Hurburgh's Austin Princess car, leaving the stolen Triumph Spitfire car behind, and went to a house, Stonewall, in Woodhouse Lane in Oxted, Surrey, 10 miles away, where they attacked a retired toy company executive, his wife and their 41-year-old son who was staying with them at the time. During the attack the son was slashed in the arm which severed his artery. The men were later acquitted of attempting to murder the son at their trial in February 1990.

After that, the gang abandoned Peter Hurburgh's Austin Princess car and then went off in the retired toy company executive's car and were said to have gone to the house of a woman in Hillyfield Lane in Fetcham, Surrey, 18 miles away, arriving at about 5.30am. They then tied her and her boyfriend up at gunpoint and robbed them, taking jewellery, credit cards, cheque books and other things. When they left, they drove off in two cars owned by the woman and her boyfriend, leaving the retired toy company executive's car behind.

Following the murder, the police released a photofit of one of the men. The police said that they thought that the murderers might have been high on drugs.

Twelve people, a woman and eleven men were arrested in dawn raids at two addresses on Monday 19 December 1988 and three of them were later charged with murder. It was reported that the police had been looking for the gang for six weeks at that point in connection with the series of other crimes, it being stated that they had already linked them to eleven other unsolved crimes. It was said that the gang had on a previous occasion raped a woman in front of her children. It was heard that the 25-year-old had blind folded the woman at her house and asked her whether she had had sex the previous night and had then put his gloved hand up her pyjama top and then fondled her genitals and then raped her next to her two year old child after which he said to her, 'I'm sorry, don't hate me'. Whilst that was going on, the gang, which had been downstairs, stole £13,000 worth of valuables from the property.

The dawn raids were carried out by Scotland Yard's PT17 Unit and the police operation to find the murderers was called 'Operation Triangle'.

Two of the men that were convicted of Peter Hurburgh's murder, the 21 and 23-year-olds, were arrested at a probation hostel in Sydenham, London whilst the third man, the 25-year-old, was not arrested until 6 January 1989 in Station Road, Dartford in Kent during what was described as a 'dramatic shootout'. He was also charged with attempting to murder a policeman as a result of the shootout although the charge was later reduced to using a firearm with intent to endanger life. When he was arrested, he had been in possession of a revolver. He was found after he hijacked three cars and was chased at high speed by the police. He was caught after he drove into Station Road near Dartford railway station in Kent which was a dead end. He jumped out of his car and climbed over a fence, during which he shot at a policeman that was chasing him. The 25-year-old was then brought to the ground with a rugby tackle.

When the police searched the probation hostel in Sydenham they found several items that had been stolen from the robberies in Woodhouse Lane, Oxted and Hillyfield Lane, Fetcham.

The police also found the 23-year-old man's fingerprints on porcelain figures at one of the houses that they had robbed on the night from which they had taken other items.

Of the other people arrested in connection with the robberies, two of them admitted to having stolen the Triumph Spitfire car, but said that they had stolen it at the request of the 21-year-old man on 13 December 1988 and that they had kept it at the probation hostel in Sydenham until the evening of 15 December 1988 at which time the 21 and 23-year-old men, and another man they did not know, but who was assumed to have been the 25-year-old man, came by and took it. The men said that they came by sometime between 11pm and midnight and asked for them to help them bump start it. The men said that the three men also asked them for balaclavas. The two men also said that they saw the 21 and 23 year-old men return later in the morning of 16 December 1988 with the stolen Renault and Vauxhall Cavalier cars along with a quantity of stolen items which they then helped to unload and hide. The two men said that they were then asked to burn the cars out as they were 'a bit warm'. It was noted that none of the men were ever charged for their parts in handling the stolen goods or disposing of the vehicles.

Shortly after the murder, the police said that whilst two of the stolen cars were found, two were still missing:

- A Blue Ford Sierra, registration E559 MHG.
- A Black Toyota Corola Coupe, registration C791 UPC.

The 21-year-old man's 16-year-old girlfriend said that the 21-year-old man had left at approximately 1.30am and had not returned until about 6.30am at which time he had been wearing different jeans and shoes and had had a Sainsbury's bag with him which was said to have been similar to one taken during the Hillyfield Lane robbery in Fetcham.

The 21-year-old man's 16-year-old girlfriend said that she saw the 21-year-old man then take several items out of the Sainsbury's bag, including:

- A pendant with a gold chain (this item was later traced to the Hillyfield Lane robbery).
- Muddied jeans.
- Muddied boots.

She added that the 21-year-old man also later gave her two rings which were later determined to have come from the Woodhouse Lane robbery in Oxted and a watch which was later found to have come from the Hillyfield Lane robbery. She was also later found to have had a watch strap that had come from the Woodhouse Lane robbery. She handed the items to the police on 19 December 1988.

When the police further searched the probation hostel in Sydenham they also found a brooch that had come from the Hillyfield Lane robbery in a waste paper basket in the 21-year-old man's room.

The 21-year-old man's girlfriend also said that when the 21-year-old man had gone out that he had been wearing a particular type of footwear and the police said that they later matched the sole impression of the footwear described with marks found at the Woodhouse Lane robbery in a flower bed and also in some blood found in the hall there.

At the time of the initial investigation it was said that the police had been inundated with calls from the public with information about the gang and that many of the leads had come from other criminals that had been sickened by their violence. The police said, 'It is certain that we have received calls from the criminal fraternity'. Rewards for information regarding the M25 Gang totalled £25,000 at the time of the arrests.

It was later determined that one of the witnesses for the prosecution had also been paid about £10,000 by the Daily Mail for his story.

At the trial it was heard that there were some weaknesses in the prosecution's case. In particular that a witness said that they had seen a green Triumph Spitfire car at 12.30am on 16 December 1988 in the spot where the stolen Triumph Spitfire car was later found which would have meant that the 21-year-old, who was said by his girlfriend to have been at the probation hostel in Sydenham at that time could not have been involved in the robberies and murder.

It was also noted by the judge during his summing up that many of the witnesses were essentially accomplices in the various crimes, including the 21-year-old man's girlfriend who had admitted to handling stolen goods.

It was also noted at the trial that there were discrepancies regarding the descriptions of the men at the various crime scenes, which was particular given that the three men convicted were all black. In the first instance, the 20-year-old man that Peter Hurburgh had been having sex with in the car had said that although the three men that had attacked them had been wearing balaclavas, that only one of them had been black and that the other two had been white.

Further, it was heard that the man and his wife from the Woodhouse Lane robbery had said that at least one of the attackers had been white, as was the case with the woman from the Hillyfield Lane robbery.

Also, before the arrests of the 21 and 23-year-old men, it was noted that the police said that they were looking for three men, one black and two white.

One of the witnesses had gone so far as to say that one of the attackers had had fair hair and blue eyes, although it was heard that at the time of the trial that the witnesses were a little vaguer about what they had seen.

It was noted that much of the prosecution's case relied on prison a confession that the 25-year-old man was said to have made to another prisoner whilst on remand in which he had used the term 'redskin' to describe one of the other men involved, it being noted that the term 'redskin' was often used by Jamaicans to describe a person with lightly coloured skin, which the 21-year-old man had.

It was also heard that there was no physical evidence linking the 25-year-old man to any of the crime scenes or to the property stolen from them.

It was noted that although much of the property stolen from the two houses in the early hours of 16 December 1988 was found at the hostel, many of the people initially arrested could have just as well have been involved in stealing it.

At the trial, the three men denied the murder or robbing the properties in Woodhouse Lane and Hillyfield Lane, but they admitted many of the other robbery charges brought against them with the 25-year-old admitting the rape of the woman as well as the robbery at her house and the 23-year-old also admitting the robbery at the woman's house.

The 25-year-old also admitted two other armed robberies on a newsagent and an off licence.

The man that was initially said to have been the third man involved in the murder by the police informant was tried at the same time on similar charges and he admitted to five burglaries in the Croydon and Dorking areas and a couple of other burglaries in Ashtead and had another 38 similar charges taken into consideration. The fourth man described himself as an honest burglar because he was not 'into people' and usually only broke into offices.

When the police raided their hostel, they said 'It was a robbers' lair. A mass of property linked to these crimes was found there'.

It was also noted that the three main prosecution witnesses, who it was noted were accomplices to parts of the crime sprees, fitted equally the descriptions of the men that murdered Peter Hurburgh. It was also noted that they had all admitted to handling items stolen from the robberies and hiding them, that they all admitted to having stolen the Triumph Spitfire car, admitted to handling the gun used in the robberies and admitted to disposing of the stolen Vauxhall and Renault cars from the Hillyfield Lane robbery.

Along with the murder, the men were convicted of a number of the other crimes and their sentences were considerable.

- The 25-year-old was sentenced to 134 years in total for his crimes which included the murder and rape as well as using a firearm with intent to endanger life.
- The 23-year-old was sentenced to an additional 64 years for his robberies and burglaries.
- The 21-year-old was sentenced to an additional 54 years for his offences.

It was also noted that all of the men had convictions dating back to their juvenile years.

When they were sentenced, the judge said, 'Just before Christmas in 1988, you struck terror into your victims in various offences of violence. You must have caused great alarm to many living in close reach to the M25 motorway in south-east London and north Surrey'.

Following their convictions, the three men appealed on 23 July 1993, and the following grounds were put forward:

- The 25-year-old man had not been identified by anyone, including the three prime witnesses who similarly matched the descriptions of the attackers.
- That there were discrepancies regarding the colour of the men seen by witnesses.
- That the man that the 25-year-old was said to have confessed to was unreliable.
- That the three primary witnesses were also themselves unreliable.
- That there was a significant discrepancy between the evidence of the 21-year-old's girlfriend regarding his movements and the Triumph Spitfire car and that of the witness that said that they had seen a green Triumph Spitfire car at the scene of the murder.

Another significant point that was raised was that of the reward money that was paid out for the information that led to the arrest of the men and the fact that the identity of the people that received it was not disclosed which it was said was vital to the case as it could have been paid out to suspects. It was also further noted that one of the three main witnesses, who could have been all also been considered suspects, was paid £10,300 by the Daily Mail in reward money, a fact that was never revealed to the jury at the trial.

However, the 23 July 1993 appeal was dismissed, with the judge saying, 'Taking all the evidence relating to the timing and events on the Thursday night and the succeeding days into account we conclude that, on the whole of the material we have reviewed, there is no basis for saying there is even a lurking doubt about the safety of the convictions of the 21-year-old and the 23-year-old, the same applies to the 25-year-old. On the contrary, the case against them all was, and remains, a formidable one'.

However, in 1997 the Criminal Cases Review Commission carried out an enquiry into the case and put forward the following points:

- One of the key witnesses was a registered police informant who had contacted his handler on 18 December 1988 about the crimes.
- Over two days of questioning, the registered police informant had alleged that the gang consisted of the 21-year-old, 23-year-old and another unemployed 18-year-old man, not the 25-year-old. It was reported on 24 December 1988 that the other man first implicated by the witness was himself later charged with a robbery in Ashstead on 9 December 1988, a burglary in Croydon on 15 December 1988, and possession of an illegal firearm. When the men were convicted, the 18-year-old, who was said to have been part of the gang of four, was described as being addicted to burglary and cocaine.
- Investigating officers had discussed the possibility of a reward being paid to him at the conclusion of the case.
- No prosecutions were carried out against any of the other witnesses who had been complicit in crimes associated with the robberies, such as handling stolen goods and stealing cars.
- One of the key witnesses was himself a known burglar with a previous conviction for robbery.
- The foreman of the jury had visited the site of the murder without the knowledge of the court. It was noted

that one of the jurors had gone to the crime scenes to see for himself, it being noted that the distance between them and the time taken to travel between them was significant and that that raised issues because he would have been basing his verdict on evidence not presented to the court which the defence would not be able to challenge.

- There was no evidence to link the 25-year-old to any of the scenes of crime or to any property stolen from them.
- Witness testimony suggested that at least one of the gang was white.
- There existed a possibility of the persons responsible for the attack upon Peter Hurburgh and his 20-year-old friend having returned to the bail hostel in the Austin Princess car before the same vehicle set off for the Napier's residence with a different team inside.

The Criminal Cases Review Commission report concluded by stating 'The new evidence and arguments create a real possibility that the 25-year-old man was not one of those three persons. Whilst there is evidence specifically linking the 21-year-old man and the 23-year-old man to the robberies, if the prosecution against one of the three, the 25-year-old man, might no longer be sustainable, in the Commission's view the Court of Appeal ought at the same time have the opportunity to consider whether the case can still be sustained against the 21-year-old man and the 23-year-old man'.

The case was next taken to the European Court of Human Rights where a judgment in respect of the 21-year-old man and the 23-year-old man found that there had been a violation of Article 6 (1) of the European Convention on Human Rights in that there had specifically been a failure to disclose the fact that one of the main witnesses was in fact a police informant at the trial. It was also noted that the police informant had also named another person as being the third man before naming the 25-year-old and that his doing so might have been as a result of the prospect of the reward.

When the case was then heard again before the court of appeal on 14 June 2000 the judge said, 'We cannot say that any of these convictions is safe. They must be quashed, and the appeals allowed. Ten years on it is not appropriate to order a retrial'. After the convictions were overturned, the judge said, 'The case against all three appellants was formidable. The evidence against the 21-year-old was overwhelming. For the better understanding of those who have listened to this judgment and of those who may report it hereafter this is not a finding of innocence, far from it'.

It was noted that the 21-year-old man went on to work for the BBC as an investigative journalist and was involved in a documentary on Barry George's conviction for the murder of Jill Dando and which was said to have been a significant factor in Barry Georges later acquittal.

Peter Hurburgh was a widowed hairdresser.

Lionel Alfonso Webb

Age: 38

Sex: male

Date: 11 Dec 1988

Place: Evering Road, Stoke Newington, London

Lionel Alfonso Webb was an estate agent with an office in 5A Evering Road, Stoke Newington and was shot at close range in his office at about 5pm on 11 December 1988.

He had been shot in the head and died from a gunshot wound to the brain fired from a shotgun.

His office had been open at the time and all the lights were on and it was said that his murder would have taken place in full view of the street.

It was thought that he had met his murderer by appointment.

It was thought that the motive might have been robbery, or a gangland hit over drugs or money. Lionel Webb was found after his death to have been in possession of a large amount of cannabis resin and amphetamines at both his office and his home.

It was also suggested that he had been murdered because of his aggressive marketing as he had been undercutting rivals, but the police developed no leads along that line of enquiry.

It was later reported that Lionel Webb was alleged to have been part of a gang of armed robbers operating out of Birmingham in the 1980s working for criminals that later went on to run large international drug operations stretching as far as Panama.

Lionel Webb was born in Barbados but had spent most of his life in Birmingham before moving down to London in 1985. He had owned a number of properties in North London.

He had recently moved his estate agency from Edgeware to Stoke Newington in

October 1988, and for weeks before that he had been supervising the refitting of the shop although it was said that even then he was scouting for new properties to buy.

It was noted that he was planning to buy the whole row of houses around his office and had made some offers to other neighbours including the woman from the yellow corner property a few doors down from his. His estate agents was opposite St Pauls Church and was called Greenvale Estate Agents and Building Contractors and he specialised in selling luxury homes abroad. He was noted as having worked seven days a week.

It was noted that five days before his death on Tuesday 6 December 1988 a white Datsun van was seen outside his office. A witness that saw the van said that they saw two men in the van, one of them with a large hook nose and a tattoo on his hand between his thumb and fingers spelling the word 'MUM'.

Lionel Webb had left his home in Mill Hill to go to work on the Sunday 11 December 1988 at about 9am. He had been carrying a briefcase and a black plastic bag.

At about 11am on the Sunday, a man wearing a dark woolly hat was seen getting out of a red car outside Lionel Webb's estate agency in Evering Road and go in.

However, it was not known what else Lionel Webb did that morning as he was not seen again until about 1.30pm when he was seen returning to his office. It was not known where he had been. It was noted that before he entered his office he looked up and down the road.

It was thought that after he entered his office he took a shower in the back area.

A short while after Lionel Webb had return, the woman that owned the yellow corner property went to his office to see him, saying that she had decided to accept his offer to buy her property for twice what she had paid for it the year before. She said that she had bought it for £36,000 in 1987 as an investment and that Lionel Webb had offered her between £75,000 and £80,000 for it. She said Lionel Webb had failed to call her back on the Thursday, saying that she had waited in all day for her to call her about it and so she went to see him about it. She said that Lionel Webb then told her that he had the money, in cash, £80,000, and told her to come by the following day when they could sign the papers.

About an hour after the woman from the corner spoke to Lionel Webb, at about 2.30pm, a man thought to have been between 50 and 60 years old was seen in Lionel Webb's office. He had been dressed in a smart trilby hat and grey chequered overcoat.

Then, at about 3pm, Lionel Webb's secretary showed up at the office saying that she had had a row with her boyfriend. It was thought that it was a surprise for Lionel Webb to see her at the office on the Sunday. She said that Lionel Webb was not in a good mood and said that when she asked him why he told her about his debts, saying that he owed £20,000 to one person, £2,000 to another person, and asked her how he was going to pay them.

His secretary said that Lionel Webb had offered to help her buy a car and that she had arranged for one to be brought to the office at about 4pm and said that when it arrived they both went out to look at it. The car owner said that Lionel Webb had offered him £4,000 for the car and asked him to wait until the end of the week for the money.

About an hour later, at about 4.50pm, a passing motorist said that he saw two white men in Lionel Webb's company at his desk in the office.

Then, at 5.30pm, a local handyman who had worked on Lionel Webb's office called in and told him that it was time that he went home and said that Lionel Webb replied something like, 'like you, I haven't got a home to go to'.

It was noted that around that time Lionel Webb then rang a friend, but the friend said that they noted that Lionel Webb didn't appear to have much to say. The woman that he called said that she then heard rustling in the background.

Also, at about the same time, two men that had been passing said that they looked into Lionel Webb's office and saw a man in a dark suit and tie sat at Lionel Webb's desk with his feet up, but said that they were confident that it wasn't Lionel Webb.

Shortly after that a black hatchback was seen to speed away from Evering Road where Lionel Webb's office was.

It was also noted that a motorist also came forward to say that they had seen a 10-year-old girl walk passed Lionel Webb's office at about 5.45pm, which the police said was a most important time and said that they wanted to speak to the girl to see if she saw anything helpful to the investigation.

Then, when the handyman returned at about the same time, 5.30pm, approximately, he said that he saw Lionel Webb's office door ajar and said that when he went in he saw that Lionel Webb had been shot at his desk.

The police said that it was possible that the motive was robbery, noting that his briefcase and £4,000 was not recovered from his office. However, they said that it was more likely that it was a gangland revenge shooting over drugs or money deals.

The police said that when they went to Lionel Webb's office, they found 2kg of cannabis resin in the back of the shop in a safe. The police said that each kilogram was wrapped up in a clear cellophane packet and added that when they went back to his home they found a large quantity of amphetamine tablets.

The police said that they had extracted shotgun pellets from the wall in the hope that they could help them identify the type of gun that had been used or where the ammunition had come from.

It was also noted that Lionel Webb had bought a house in his girlfriend's name without her knowledge.

His inquest returned a verdict of unlawful killing by persons unknown.

A retired detective later said in 2009 that he had been part of a police operation to watch a known armed robber case out a bank in Harborne in 1986 along with his several henchmen, one of whom was alleged to have been Lionel Webb. The retired detective said that he watched the gang casing the bank for over three weeks, but said that they moved in and made some arrests before they robbed the bank, seizing 1kg of cocaine from the gang leaders large house along with a suitcase containing about £13,000 worth of burned banknotes. It was said that although the leader was convicted of drugs offences, that the rest of the gang, including Lionel Webb, were acquitted after they claimed that they had only been meeting up to discuss a drug deal.

The detective described the gang as ruthless and said that they were premier league and would not stop to hesitate before shooting anyone that got in their way. The detective noted however that although the gang split up, none of them prospered, with one of them being convicted for a failed armed robbery in Redditch in which he shot at a policeman and was sentenced to 25 years, another ending up in a Panamanian prison where he had run an international drugs network and Lionel Webb being shot in the head two years later shortly after leaving Birmingham.

The detective noted that at the time, in the latter part of the 1980s that many organised criminals were moving away from armed robberies and into drugs which up until then had been dominated by public schoolboys and hippies.

John Heron

Age: 35

Sex: male

Date: 9 Dec 1988

Place: British Rail Travel Centre, Waterloo Station, London

John Heron was stabbed in the back in the British Rail Travel Centre at Waterloo Station in London on the night of Friday 9 December 1988 at about 8.45pm.

He was stabbed by a man that wrongly accused him of jumping the queue.

After being stabbed he was taken to St Thomas's Hospital in London but suffered from a heart attack as a result of being stabbed and died. John Heron had suffered stab injuries to his lungs and arms.

John Heron had been waiting in line at the time to get information about trains from London to Glasgow.

His attacker was described as being white, aged between 30 and 40, between 5ft 6in and 5ft 9in tall, of a medium proportionate build, with a long, thin face, and dark straggly greasy brown collar length hair. He was said to have been wearing a light grey jacket and to have been scruffy. Two photofits of the man was released. The police later said that they thought that his attacker was Scottish and that he was back in Scotland and probably being shielded.

The police said that they were also anxious to speak to a man that had been standing in front of the attacker in the queue who had been making lengthy inquiries at the centre shortly before John Heron was stabbed. The police said, 'This man was in front of the attacker and may have seen him close up. He may have vital information as to his capture. It is possible the attacker had a Scottish accent, a casual worker like Mr Heron who had come down south to work'.

In March 1989 the police said that they were trying to trace two men who they thought could help to track down John Heron's murderer.

The first was thought to have been a road manager with a rock group. He was described as being about 30 to 40 years old, about 5ft 8in tall, and to have come from Kilbirnie near Glasgow. The police said that they thought that he might have 'important information' about John Heron's murder and said that they thought that he had been working in the London area for about two years.

The second man, who was named, was aged about 40 and had been drinking in the Skinners Arms pub in Southwark on the night of the murder. It was said that he was thought to have been with a group of people that had been drinking there and had been talking to the other man thought to have been a road manager from Kilbirnie. The police noted that he was not a suspect.

John Heron was from Barrhead in Glasgow but had left his wife in Glasgow to go to Bracknell to get work as a heating engineer and it was thought that he was on his way back home when he was murdered. He had been living in Tebbit Close in Bracknell at the time.

John Heron was an ex-paratrooper and was married with three children.

Harry Howell

Age: 74

Sex: male

Date: 22 Nov 1988

Place: Ibbison Court, Blackpool, Lancashire

Harry Howell was found dead in his home in Ibbison Court in Blackpool. He had been beaten about the head with a blunt instrument and robbed.

He was last seen on the Guy Fawkes weekend on Saturday 5 November 1988.

His body was found in his chair in the living room of his flat two weeks later on 22 November 1988. It was noted that he had been dead for 17 days. The murder weapon was never found.

His wife had died four weeks earlier.

He had been living in sheltered accommodation for elderly people at the time he was murdered in Ibbison Court and a warden would go round each day to check on the elderly residents. He had previously suffered a stroke that had partly paralysed him, and he was blind in one eye and also slightly deaf.

Shortly after his wife died, his son met him at her funeral and spoke to him about his care and then later took him to the Newgate Cafe in Central Drive, Blackpool, which was very near to where he lived and spoke to a waitress there and explained Harry Howell's situation to her and explained that he would be going there once a day from then on and said that he was to get a proper meal each day, stressing that he wasn't to be eating sandwiches.

Although Harry Howell was elderly and had suffered from a stroke, he was described as being an independent type who enjoyed placing a bet and having a pint and said that he had recently started to drink in The George public house on Central Drive which was around the corner from his home, and the police said that they were interested in speaking to anyone that had seen anyone talking to Harry Howell there. It was also noted that he also drank in the Brunswick in Bonny Street and the Royal Oak in South Shore.

However, it was noted that he used to carry a large amount of money in his wallet and that he would make a point of telling people that he was well off. It was also noted that he had kept his life savings at his flat as he didn't trust banks and that he would often talk about that. However, it was noted that when the police searched Harry Howell's flat they found £2,000 and found another £1,100 on his person indicating that after killing Harry Howell, his murderer had taken his wallet and watch but had not searched him or his flat.

However, the police said that they thought that the motive behind his murder was money.

Harry Howell was last seen by the warden at Ibbison Court at 9.30am on the Saturday 5 November 1988.

An hour later he went to the Newgate Cafe for his breakfast which was then his usual routine.

Whilst there, a waitress said that she remembered serving a well-dressed man there that she hadn't seen before and said that he bought a cup of tea and went and sat at the same table that Harry Howell was sitting at and that they sat there talking for a while. The police said that they were interested in speaking to the well-dressed man. The man was described as:

- Tall.
- Broadly built.
- Wearing a fawn coloured overcoat and trilby hat

At about the same time a man went into Burtons Bakery on Central Drive in Blackpool where Harry Howell usually bought a pie each lunchtime and said that he had come in for some meat sandwiches for an old-man that came in there regularly and asked whether the shop assistant knew him. He explained that he wanted meat sandwiches but when he was told that they didn't have any he bought two beef and horseradish sandwiches. The two beef and horseradish sandwiches were later found unopened in their packaging and the Burtons Bakery paper bag they had been put in in Harry Howell's flat. It was noted that the two beef and horseradish sandwiches were the only beef and horseradish sandwiches that the bakery had made and sold on 5 November 1988.

The man that had gone into the bakery was described as having dark hair and the police later released a photofit of him. His full description was:

- Aged in his 30s.
- Tall.
- Slim.
- Pale drawn face.
- Dark hair that fell over his face/forehead.

It was noted that Harry Howell enjoyed speaking to people and that on the Saturday afternoon at about 4pm he met two strangers in Blackpool in the street, a man and woman with two young children who he kept speaking for about 20 minutes. It was noted that he told them that he had no financial worries as he had plenty of money stashed away.

It was noted that Harry Howell didn't mix much with the other people in Ibbison Court and it was not known whether he had spent Guy Fawkes night alone or not.

The following morning the milkman delivered a pint of milk to Harry Howell's flat which was later taken in by someone.

It was noted that the warden used an internal intercom to check on the residents on Sundays and that she said that when she spoke to him on the morning of Sunday 6 November 1988 that he told her that he was fine.

When the warden went round to see the residents on the Monday morning 7 November 1988 she saw that Harry Howell had placed a piece of white card in the window of his front door which it was said was a system that residents used to signify that they had gone out for a while and so she didn't knock and went on about her rounds.

On Tuesday 8 November 1988 the milk man called at about 7.30am and left a pint of milk and noted that the white card was still in the door glass.

Later that day, at about 8.30am, the home help sent by the Social Services went to see Harry Howell and noticed that there was a note on his door addressed to the milk man saying that he was on holiday for two weeks and asking that no milk was delivered. The note read, 'On Holiday for 2 weeks. No Milk Please'. However, it was noted that the milkman who had been there an hour earlier had not seen it. About 30 minutes after the home help had been there the deputy warden passed by on her regular round and she said that she didn't any note on the door.

It was thought that the note had only been on the door for 30 minutes and the police said that there was no indication that Harry Howell had been planning on going on holiday and that it was probable that his murderer had put it there and then removed it shortly after.

It was additionally heard that a window cleaner that came by later that afternoon didn't see a note pinned to Harry Howell's front door either when he washed the glass in Harry Howell's front door and it was not known what had happened to it. The window cleaner said that as he was working that he soon after saw a young man go up to Harry Howell's front door and knock, but said that he didn't get a reply and then walked off. He described the man as:

- Aged in his 40s.
- About 5ft 7in tall.

On Thursday 10 November 1988 the milkman called again and after he saw the pint that he had left on the Tuesday still on the doorstep he thought that Harry Howell had gone away without telling him and so took the bottle of milk away.

It was noted that it wasn't until twelve days later that it was noticed that something was wrong.

It was on Tuesday 22 November 1988 that the window cleaner went round again and whilst he was washing the glass pane in Harry Howell's front door he noticed that the doorframe had been damaged although the door was still firmly locked. The window cleaner said that he became concerned and so wen to the back of the flat and used his ladder to look through the window and saw Harry Howell's body lying in his armchair in his lounge.

It was noted that there was quite a bit of damage to his front door and that it was surprising that no one had noticed it before. However, the police said that whilst it indicated that there had been a burglary, they said that it might have been caused later to cover up for a burglary.

It was noted that quite a few things had been stolen from Harry Howell's flat, including:

- A gold watch with a gold rim. It was said that it had something like 'To Harry Flegg On His Retirement' inscribed on the back.
- 12 keys to his home.
- A brown wallet. It was noted that it was known that in the past Harry Howell had kept about £700 in the wallet.
- Bus pass.

Harry Howell had previously worked for British Leyland.

The police later said that his murder was similar to that of Jack Shuttleworth who was murdered in his shed in Ingleton on 3 August 1989 by a man that had won his confidence. However, the main suspect in Jack Shuttleworth's case later hung himself in Armley prison whilst on remand.

Bernard Cole

Age: 45

Sex: male

Date: 22 Nov 1988

Place: New Park Court, Brixton Hill, Brixton

Bernard Cole was shot in the face in New Park Court, Brixton Hill in the early hours of 22 November 1988.

A 25-year-old unemployed heating engineer was tried twice for his murder but found not guilty. His first trial ended in a hung jury whilst he was acquitted of both murder and manslaughter at the second trial.

Bernard Cole was a nightclub bouncer and was shot at point blank range in the face as he was getting into his car in New Park Court after finishing work.

It was said that the man had confessed to the murder twice, but he denied that saying that the confessions were completely false and that at the time of the murder he had been at his parents' house asleep.

The court heard that the man tried, described as a frail 5ft 2in tall man had shot Bernard Cole with a primitive highwayman's gun after he had failed to kill him with poison and a hand grenade. It was claimed that the man had shot Bernard Cole after Bernard Cole, who was described as a womaniser, had sexually assaulted his girlfriend and tried to seduce his girlfriend's sister.

Bernard Cole had lived in Holmwood Road in Brixton Hill, London.

Sarfraz Ahmed

Age: 30

Sex: male

Date: 15 Nov 1988

Place: Peterbrough, Cambridgeshire

Sarfraz Ahmed was found stabbed to death in his taxi-cab.

His body was found in his cab in a remote country lane about eight miles away from his base in Cambridgeshire by a farmworker.

Nothing more is known.

James Gibson

Age: 23

Sex: male

Date: 15 Nov 1988

Place: Alderville Road, Walton, Merseyside

James Gibson was shot at point blank range on Tuesday 15 November 1988.

He was shot yards from his home in Alderville Road in Walton. He had lived in Baythorne Road.

A man was seen getting into a black car shortly after and a photofit was made of him. The man was described as:

- In his late 20s.
- About 5ft 10in tall.
- Muscular build.

The day after the murder, the police found a black MG Maestro car abandoned a mile and a half away in Clubmoor. Its registration number was B809 GUP and it was determined to have been stolen five days earlier in Chester. The police appealed for anyone that knew where the car might have been kept in the five days between it being stolen and it being found abandoned.

It was said that James Gibson had not known what had hit him and that he had slumped to the pavement with his hands still in his pockets after being shot.

It was later heard at a trial in 1989 that James Gibson had been involved in a bank robbery at a National Westminster Bank in Preston in which £500,000 had been stolen. The other man involved in the bank robbery was described as an armed robber and kidnapper. However, it was heard that both James Gibson and the armed robber were actually minnows in the crime and that there had been a gang of six men behind the robbery who had pulled the strings and that it was thought that they might hold the clues as to why James Gibson was shot. However, the men were not traced.

It was said that James Gibson might have been shot in a gangland killing to silence him about the robbery or that he had had underworld drug dealing connections.

The armed robber was jailed for 13 years. However, he refused to name any names of the other people involved for fear of reprisals. He was convicted of robbery, kidnap, false imprisonment and the possession of a sawn-off shotgun.

The armed robber had been arrested soon after James Gibson was murdered after he was spotted in the grounds of Fazakerley Hospital where £12,000 and two balaclavas had been buried.

After James Gibson was murdered, his family described him as 'a man with no enemies'.

Derek Brann

Age: 49

Sex: male

Date: 6 Nov 1988

Place: M20, Sellinge, Kent

Derek Brann was found dead on the side of the M20 in Kent on 20 November 1988 having been killed with a sharp instrument.

He had been stabbed 34 times and his murder was described as having been violent and frenzied. It was thought that the motive was robbery and that between £50 and £60 was stolen from him.

He was working as a taxi-cab driver at the time and it was thought that he had been murdered by a person that he had picked up in Folkestone over the Guy Fawkes weekend, 5 to 6 November 1988.

His taxi cab was found by a member of the public at about 11.45am on Sunday 6 November 1988 at the bottom of Horn Street in Seabrook, Hythe and his body was found two weeks later on 20 November 1988 on the M20 near Sellinge on the London bound carriageway behind a crash barrier by a motorist that broke down on the hard shoulder.

However, Derek Brann's taxi had been seen by the barmaid from the Fountain public house which was at the bottom of Horn Street at 12.20am on Sunday 6 November 1988 as she went home. She said that she had been trying to get taxi-cabs for her customers all night and found that they were exceptionally busy because of Guy Fawkes night with 30 minute waits and that as she went home she saw Derek Brann's taxi in the layby where it was found later that day, empty, and noted the irony that all the while she had been trying to get a taxi-cab there had been one sat right outside.

His taxicab, a red Nissan Bluebird 2.0LX, registration C180 GKE, was covered with blood inside across the backseats and it was thought that his murderer would have also been covered in blood and the police appealed for anyone that knew of anyone coming home following bonfire night on 6 November 1988 with blood on their clothing to come forward.

It was noted that the forensic analysts had said that they had found two types of blood in Derek Brann's taxi and believed that the murderer had cut themselves in the frenzied attack.

Although the barmaid from the Fountain public house said she had seen Derek Brann's taxicab in the layby near the pub at 12.20am, it was also reported that Derek Brann had been flagged down in Beachborough Road, Folkestone, in the early hours of 6 November 1988 between 2am and 2.30am and called it in to his taxi controller saying that he was taking someone to St Martin's Plain to the west of Folkestone. As such, it was not known why Derek Brann had been dumped near Sellinge and the killer had then returned towards Folkestone to leave the car at the bottom of Horn Street where it was found the following day, and it was thought that the murderer might have lived nearby or known someone nearby.

When Derek Brann's taxi was found there was a £22.70 fare on the meter which the police said indicated that it had travelled about 31.5 miles.

The police also said that the front wheels were covered in mud and as such decided to search the Romney Marsh area first.

Before his body was found, on Friday 18 November 1988, the Daily Mirror published an article linking his disappearance with the murders of three other taxi drivers, John Landa in August 1982, Noel Smith in June 1988 and Sarfraz Ahmed in November 1988 and suggested that they had all been murdered by a maniac knifeman that bore a grudge against taxi-drivers. All three men had been stabbed to death in their cabs and the article stated that the police were linking Derek Brann's disappearance at the time to their murders.

Derek Brann was married with three sons. His main job was as an insurance salesman, but he had recently started driving taxi-cabs in the evenings and weekends to earn more money and had been doing it for about six weeks.

He had been working for the Folkestone Taxi company at the time of his murder and had been sharing his taxi-cab with two other drivers.

Derek Brann had started work on Saturday 5 November 1988 at about 1pm, taking over from one of the other drivers that had been driving the cab in the morning so that he could do the afternoon and evening shifts. It was said that it had been a quiet afternoon and Derek Brann had gone home at 8.30pm for his supper which he had with his wife. He told her that the afternoon had been quiet but that he expected the night to be busy and didn't expect to be getting home until about 3am Sunday 6 November 1988.

Derek Brann was later seen by another taxi-driver outside the Burstin Hotel at Folkestone Harbour waiting in the taxi-rank there at about 10pm.

It was thought that Derek Brann might have been seen next at 10.20pm by a security guard in Middleburg Square who said that he saw two men get into what he thought was Derek Brann's taxi.

The police said that they knew of no further sightings of Derek Brann, however, it was also reported that he had called into his office at between 2am and 2.30am on 6 November 1988 to say he had picked up a fare in St Martin's Plain for west of Folkestone, but that detail was omitted from other accounts of the case and contradicts the sighting of his cab at the bottom of Horn Street at 12.20am 6 November 1988 or other accounts of his taxi-cab being seen on the M20 near Sellinge.

The police suggested that it was possible that Derek Brann had been stabbed by a customer who had then determined to take him to a hospital, the nearest of which was in Ashford and had gone along the M20 to do so but that for some reason had then stopped and dumped his body before returning to the Folkestone area.

The police added that they did not think that Derek Brann would have driven his taxi out along the M20 as it was standard practice for him to call into his taxi office to say if he was leaving the Folkestone area and that as such they thought that it was safe to assume that the murderer had driven the taxi there.

The police said that they knew that Derek Brann's taxi had stopped where his body was dumped on the M20 because a couple that had driven past later said that they had seen it at about 10.30pm. One of them said that they had thought that it was the police, 'the old bill' and warned the driver but that the driver had corrected them by pointing out that it wasn't a police car but a taxi. They added that they later saw the taxi turn off at junction 10, about 5 miles further along the M20.

It was later noted that when Derek Brann's taxi was seen parked up on the hard shoulder of the M20 that a white van was also seen parked up very closely behind it, a matter of feet. The police appealed for the driver of the white van to come forward and suggested that he might have simply stopped after having seen the taxi-cab pulled over on the hard shoulder with its hazard lights on to see if they could assist.

It was noted that at about the same time witnesses saw a man walking along the M20 back towards the Folkestone area and the police said that they thought that Derek Brann had been attacked by multiple people and that the man seen walking along the M20 was one of the attackers who had got out of the taxi after they had dumped Derek Brann's body over the side, possibly having had a disagreement with the other assailants over what had happened and having wanted to immediately disassociate himself from what had taken place by getting out of the taxi-cab and walking home.

It was further noted that Derek Brann's was later seen in the Romney Marsh area shortly after 11pm. The person that saw it said that he drove about that area frequently and seldom saw other cars about at that time and thought to himself that it was really unusual to see a Folkestone taxi out on the Romney Marsh.

Derek Brann's taxi was next seen at about 11.15pm at the bottom of Horn Street. It was noticed as it had been driving along Seabrooke Road and had appeared to have missed the Horn Street junction and overshot it and so had reversed back so that it could turn into Horn Street where it was later found dumped. The person that saw Derek Brann's taxi overshoot Horn Street said that they got a very good look at the driver and a photofit of the suspect was released.

Anthony Beyit

Age: 24

Sex: male

Date: 25 Oct 1988

Place: Ladbroke Grove Tube Station,
Thorpe Close, Notting Hill

Anthony Beyit was murdered outside a pub
by three men who thought he had stolen a
jacket from a pub. However, it was said that
he was the victim of mistaken identity.

A 19-year-old actor who had been in 30
episodes of the Children's television
program Grange Hill was tried for his
murder but acquitted. He was also acquitted
of affray but was convicted of attempting to
pervert the course of justice after it was
found that he had arranged for several
people to give him a false alibi.

There had been a fight earlier on at the Elgin
Pub in Ladbroke Grove during which a coat
was stolen by another drinker on the night of
25 October 1988. During the fight windows

in the pub were broken and bottles and glasses were thrown.

It was said that a group of drinkers then went out to look for the man and found Anthony Beyit who they punched, kicked, beat with a stick and stabbed in Thorpe Close, Notting Hill by Ladbroke Grove Tube Station.

A witness said that she looked out of her window and saw Anthony Beyit curled into a ball as he was being attacked with fists and feet by three men.

Following the attack, the three men walked away and Anthony Beyit then staggered off to a shop from where he was then taken to hospital where he died from his injuries and shock about two hours later. He had suffered two knife wounds that had pierced his liver.

The 19-year-old actor who had initially lied about where he had been at the time of the murder later admitted to having had been in Thorpe Close at the time of the murder, but said that he had had nothing to do with the fight. He said that he saw Anthony Beyit fighting a man that he only knew as Bones. He said that he then ran away after hearing a shout.

The 19-year-old actor said that he then made up his alibi as he was scared because he was facing a murder charge. He had arranged for his girlfriend, his brother and a friend to say that they had all been celebrating his and his girlfriend's anniversary together. However, his girlfriend later broke down whilst she was being questioned by the police and told them the truth.

He had spent four and a half months on remand and so was released after he was convicted of intending to pervert the course of justice. He was also given a community service order.

Anthony Beyit had been living in Sable Street, Islington at the time.

It was later reported in February 1991 that it had been Anthony Beyit's dying wish that his sister look after his dog. However, she was later made homeless, along with the dog after she was told to leave the hostel where she had been staying because they didn't allow animals there and she went to see a housing clerk at a branch of the neighbourhood offices to ask for new accommodation. She then had a row over her situation and assaulted the clerk there, pulling her hair and pouring coffee over her.

She was convicted for assault at the Highbury Magistrates and given 12-months probation and ordered to pay £20 compensation to the clerk.

Ho Ay Long

Age: 16

Sex: male

Date: 25 Oct 1988

Place: River Thames, Southbank, London

Ho Ay Long was found floating in the River Thames near the Southbank in London at 9.30pm on Tuesday 25 October 1988.

He had been strangled.

He was last seen alive the previous evening, Monday 24 October 1988, leaving his home in North Peckham.

When his body was pulled out of the river, he had been wearing beige trousers and a black cropped vest with a spider in a spider web motif on the front and back and was bare foot. However, it was noted that when he had left home he had been wearing a brown leather flying jacket over his clothes and a pair of trainers.

It was said that when he was pulled out of the river, he had not been in the water for more than 30 minutes.

Linda Donaldson

Age: 31

Sex: female

Date: 18 Oct 1988

Place: Winwick Lane, Lowton, Manchester

Linda Donaldson was found dead and mutilated in a ditch 18 miles away from her home.

It was thought that she might have been murdered and mutilated by more than one person and possibly in response to a television program the day before on Jack the Ripper.

She had been stabbed multiple times and mutilated and the police described her murder as a 'Jack the Ripper' style killing. The police said, 'An attempt had been made to remove her head by severing it at the neck'.

The police said that they were not ruling out the possibility that her murderer had been a regular client.

She had been a prostitute and had lived and worked in the Canning Street red light district in Toxteth, also known as 'The Square'. It was noted that many of the women working the streets were there for one reason, and that was heroin and they many of them were drug addicts and had turned to prostitution to fund their needs.

However, it was said that she was a really friendly person and that everyone liked her.

Her working name was Tracy which was the name that most of her customers would have known her by.

It was said that although she was a prostitute, she was careful in a number of ways and regularly visited a nearby clinic set up to prevent the spread of aids where she would pick up free needles and condoms.

It was also noted that she would take her clients back home via a back alleyway so as not to offend neighbours. It was noted that she had been invited to appear on the Kilroy television show in December 1987 about prostitution where she had talked about that very issue, saying that she would not like to live with her children where prostitutes were bringing men home. In the television program, she had said, 'Are we supposed to work on a deserted street and get mugged and raped and maybe attacked?'. She also said, 'The police in Liverpool wanted us to work on a deserted street in front of the Cathedral, and then they thought about it a bit more and they put us back in a residential area because it was less dangerous'. She then said, 'I certainly don't walk past when someone's got kids around. I wouldn't dream of chatting up a man right in front of kids. Not many girls will'.

The police said, 'She was somebody who realised the dangers. From what we have been told she was not the sort of girl prepared to go with just anybody. She was very, very careful about choosing her clients'.

On the night of Monday 17 October 1988 from 7pm, Linda Donaldson had been on her regular spot on the corner of Canning Street and Catharine Street. It was said that she was distinctive because she had always worn black.

It was noted that at some time before 10pm she had visited a shop in Windsor Street to buy some groceries. which was described as being part of her normal routine and that after doing her shopping she had returned to her flat to feed her pets. She had a dog and three cats which her flatmate had rescued as strays from the streets.

It was noted that she walked everywhere quickly.

However, by 11pm it was said that she was back on the streets at the corner of Canning Street and Catharine Street to meet customers. She was spotted by two plain clothed policemen at about 11pm talking to a man. One of the plain clothed policemen said that he knew Linda Donaldson.

Although it was described as a quiet night, it was said that Linda Donaldson had met a number of clients.

Another prostitute that had been working in Grove Street said that at about 11.30pm she was approached by a man whose behaviour made her feel uneasy. She said that he asked her if she was doing business and then asked her if she knew anywhere dark. She said that the man had had a bag with him that made a clanking sound when he put it down. However, the police said that they were unable to trace the man. However, a photofit of the man was released. The man was described as:

- 5ft 11in tall.
- Aged in his late 20s.
- Wearing a white polo neck sweater.

About two hours later at 1.30am in the early hours of Tuesday 18 October 1988 the prostitute that had met the man with the clunking bag met Linda Donaldson and said that they talked about business and said that she told her about the weird man that she had met after which she hailed a taxi to go home. However, she said that as the taxi pulled away, she noticed Linda Donaldson moving off towards a dark car that had just come by which had pulled into back Canning Street. However, it was never determined who had been in the car and no one saw her alive again.

Another prostitute said that she had seen a man approach Linda Donaldson twice on the night she was murdered. She said 'He approached Linda twice that evening, as late as midnight. Each time she didn't want anything to do with him'. She described the man as:

- Between 6ft and 6ft 2in tall.
- Aged 42 to 45 years.
- Thin build.
- Wearing gold rimmed square spectacles, a green quilted old-fashioned anorak, a crew-neck jumper and dark trousers.
- Facial features including dimples on either side of his thin, longish face when he smiled.
- Mid-brown hair, going grey and parted at the right-hand side with both sides brushed back. The prostitute said that it appeared to be either a smart haircut but could possibly have been a wig and was in a fixed position.
- His appearance tended towards the untidy.
- He wore a silver coloured watch on his left wrist.

Her flatmate reported her missing later on 18 October 1988 and her body was found by an elderly couple later that afternoon.

About four hours later, between 5.45am and 6.45am on Tuesday 18 October 1988, about 18 miles away, a maroon Ford Grenada Mark 2 car was seen parked in Winwick Lane near Leigh and it was thought that the people in the car might have seen something suspicious as it was not far from where Linda Donaldson's body was later found.

Later that day, at about lunch time, an elderly couple in a car pulled off of the M6 motorway at junction 22 and joined the A579 road to Leigh and soon after at about 1.30pm pulled in to the same place where the maroon Ford Grenada had been seen earlier. The woman said that because they had been driving for a while, she would get stiff and liked to stop and stretch her legs. They said that when they pulled over into the field entrance and walked about, they saw what they thought was a body. The man then went over and found that it was a body and it was later determined to be the body of Linda Donaldson.

Linda Donaldson's body was naked when it was found. She had been stabbed to death and mutilated.

The police said that they thought that Linda Donaldson had been picked up, murdered, her body mutilated and that she had then been dumped in the location where she was found. They said that she had been murdered elsewhere and then dumped in the ditch.

However, the police said that they had no idea where she had been murdered, but stated that it was quite clear that the murderer had had plenty of room to carry out the murder and the mutilation and that it was likely that the place where she had been murdered was someplace between Liverpool and Winwick Lane. The police added that they thought that the murderer had also had plenty of light and had taken their time over the murder.

Her clothing, including a black dress, and handbag were never found.

The police said that they were also still trying to trace the murder weapon which they said they thought had been a heavy bladed knife that was at least 8 inches long.

It was noted that earlier on the 17 October 1988, the day before Linda Donaldson was found, there had been an airing on the television of a Jack the Ripper dramatisation starring the famous actor Michael Caine which took place 100 years after the Jack the Ripper murders in London and it was speculated that the program had prompted someone to carry out a similar murder, resulting in Linda Donaldson's murder and mutilation.

The police said, 'We are looking for a maniac, a sadistic killer who could strike again. The type of man who could do this to another human being defies description. The mutilation was probably done in a bid to conceal identity'.

It was later reported on 25 October 1988 that the police received a report from another prostitute in Liverpool who said that she had been confronted by a knifeman in Liverpool. She said that the incident happened in the early hours of Sunday 23 October 1988. It was reported that she had fled for help from someone in a parked car after the knifeman had put the knife to her throat and had demanded his money back. The police said that the alleged incident had happened at about 2.30am near the university buildings in Mount Pleasant.

The police said that they were running a 'crime pattern analysis' to check with other police forces to see if there were any similarities with other murders or attacks in the country. It was reported that the police had put together a team of 250 officers in the hunt for her murderer.

The police said that they had interviewed 415 kerb crawlers, identified 103 of Linda

Donaldson's former clients, spoken to just under 10,000 people and examined 6,000 cars during their investigation. The police noted that one of the problems with the investigation was the fact that many of the men that picked up prostitutes in the red-light district came from outside the Merseyside area.

The police later arrested a person inside Liverpool Magistrates court in relation to her murder, but they later released him without charge.

They said that they were also interested in speaking to an anonymous caller that called the incident room on the Sunday night 6 November 1988 but then rang off.

They said that they were also interested in tracing two of Linda Donaldson's known clients, both said to have been businessmen and to have been well off, one of them driving a Jaguar XJS. The police said that one of the men was Linda Donaldson's Tuesday visitor and the other was a regular client that Linda Donaldson would see on Thursdays. The police said that they were interested in the men coming forward so that they could be eliminated from their inquiries. The police added that they believed they knew the identity of the two men but wanted to give them the chance to come forward voluntarily to save them the embarrassment of them calling at their homes.

Linda Donaldson was divorced and shared a flat with a friend but was said to have kept in regular contact with her family. It was said that she had been born and educated in Crosby 'to a reasonably high standard'.

Laurence Winstanley

Age: 24

Sex: male

Date: 2 Oct 1988

Place: Baitings Dam, Littleborough, Ripponden, West Yorkshire

Laurence Winstanley was shot in the head after havng been partly burned and mutilated.

His body was found in Baitings Dam, just off the A58, wrapped up in a curtain and weighed down with a pick-axe head about a year after he vanished on 26 September 1989. At the time his body was found the water level in the dam had been unusually low due to the hot summer.

At the time of his murder the police said that they thought that it was a targetted gangland execution and said that they thought that more than one person had been involved.

The police said that it appeared that an attempt had been made to burn his body.

He had lived in Ogden, Rochdale with his family but had previously lived in Cliff Hill Road in Shaw, Oldham the previous year and was a part-time car dealer and car mechanic with his own garage, New Start Autos, in Sholver, Oldham.

On the night that he vanished he had been out to a local pub, The Windsor, where it was heard that he received a telephone call that seemed to worry him. After that it was heard that he went off to his mother's house in Shaw which was a few minutes away, but that the journey took him over an hour. The police said that they were interested in finding out what he did during that hour.

After visiting his mother he then went back to the pub for a while but was never seen again. No one was sure what time he left after his return.

Two days after Laurence Winstanley vanished, on 4 October 1988, a man giving the name of Burrows took Laurence Winstanley's red Ford Cortina estate car, registration number SAT 385W, to a scrap yard in Milnrow, Oldham, but the man was never traced. It was noted that Laurence Winstanley had recently bought the car for £350 and had been planning to sell it for £800 and so wouldn't have scrapped it.

During their investigation, the police raided several homes in Rochdale and Littleborough in January 1990 and a man was questioned, no arrests were made.

In December 2016 the police searched a pond near Blackstone Edge Road in Littleborough for clues.

Albert Smith

Age: 60

Sex: male

Date: 23 Sep 1988

Place: Carterhatch Road, Enfield, London

Albert Smith was found dead at his home in Carterhatch Road, Enfield on 23 September 1987.

He had been throttled.

A 23-year-old man was tried for his murder at the Old Bailey but the judge ordered the jury to return a not guilty verdict after stating that the evidence was too risky for a jury to convict him.

The man tried was dubbed the 'Mohican-Haired Murderer' because shortly after the murder he had got a Mohican style haircut.

It was claimed that the 23-year-old man had throttled Albert Smith with his tie which stopped his heart from beating.

The prosecution said that the 23-year-old man had been one of a gang of builders that had been working at Albert Smith's house a few days before his murder and that he had gone back to Albert Smith's house sometime between 18 and 21 September 1988 and because Albert Smith had recognised him he had let him in and that the 23-year-old man had then killed him.

A pathologist from Charing Cross Hospital said that Albert Smith had been a paranoid schizophrenic which meant that he would have been more likely than other people to have taken his own life. He said that whilst it was unlikely that Albert Smith had committed suicide, he said that he could not rule out the possibility.

The post mortem heard that his larynx was fractured, but it was stated that because of his age that his larynx would have been more brittle. It was further noted that there were only slight markings on his skin.

The pathologist added that he thought that Albert Smith had most likely died when his tie was twisted and tightened around his neck, resulting in his heart stopping.

When the judge heard the medical evidence, he said that he was worried by it stating that the pathologists conclusions meant that the medical evidence was unreliable.

The judge also noted that he was also worried by other contradictory evidence between that of the prosecution and defence regarding the time that a defence witness said that they had seen Albert Smith alive and that of the milkman who gave evidence for the prosecution who said that Albert Smith must have been dead at the same time as he had not picked up the two pints of milk from his doorstep which he had left the previous day.

The judge noted that the only significant evidence that the prosecution had submitted was that of a man that said that the 23-year-old man had confessed to the murder to him as they drank together in the Golden Hind public house in Enfield.

It was also heard that the 23-year-old man had totally changed his appearance overnight and had given himself a Mohican style haircut from which he had got his nickname. However, when he appeared in court he had a normal haircut.

It was also heard that following his arrest, it was found that his fingerprints matched prints found at Albert Smith's house on a bowl, but the defence said that he could have left them there when he had been at Albert Smith's house a few days earlier working there with the gang of builders.

After the judge heard the evidence, he said, 'It would be quite unsafe to allow you to even think of reaching a verdict' and the 23-year-old man was acquitted.

David Terence Short

Age: 36

Sex: male

Date: 22 Sep 1988

Place: 2 Ethel Road, Broadstairs, Kent

David Terence Short was murdered at his house in Ethel Road on the evening of Thursday 22 September 1988.

He answered his door and someone sprayed CS gas in his eyes incapacitating him and he was then hit over the head twice with some object and died soon after.

He had lived in Broadstairs Kent and had done so for most of his life. At the time he had been working as a double-glazing salesman for Danham Windows as their East Kent representative and had been doing so since Christmas 1987.

It was noted that he had done a variety of jobs over the years and that in 1996 he had been working at the Castle Keep hotel as a barman. It was said that one night whilst he was working there that two men came in and threatened to kill him if there was any more trouble from him and that a week later he turned up for work with two black eyes and a swollen face.

The police noted that David Short used to frequent a number of the nightclubs around Broadstairs and said that they were interested in speaking to anyone that had seen him in any of them. It was also said that he had become associated with a person called Maz, but the police said that they didn't know who that was and had never traced him.

It was noted that business was going very well for David Short and he bought a distinctive white Rover car. However, it was damaged around the time of his death as though someone had attacked it and about a month before his death someone had vandalised his car with paint stripper and it was concluded that someone had a grudge against him and knew where he lived.

It was noted that there were also three other incidents:

1. A red cross had been painted on his door.
2. Funeral wraths had been delivered to his home.
3. He had received a number of malicious telephone calls.

Two weeks before he was murdered a neighbour said that they looked out of their window and noticed a short dark-haired man arguing with David Short on his doorstep. At the time she said that she thought that it perhaps had something to do with his business. The police later released a photofit of the man who also had a moustache.

On the day he was murdered, Thursday 22 September 1988, David Short had come home from an afternoon appointment and had prepared the evening meal which he had with his wife and his mother at their dining room table at about 5.30pm. David Short and his wife had been planning on buying a new house together and they had a discussion about it.

At about 7pm a neighbour said that she saw David Short's wife and mother leaving the house to go off and play bingo. She said that she next saw David Short leave his house about ten minutes later at 7.10pm, smartly dressed and carrying a briefcase. She said that she noted that David Short had sat in his car for a few minutes before driving off.

The police said that David Short's diary indicated that he had had an appointment in Deal, Kent at that time and it was thought to have been about 8.45pm when he had returned home.

When he got back there was a yellow Vauxhall Chevette parked across the road from his house which had broken down and the owner had gone off for help.

Shortly after, at about 9.15pm a witness saw a motorcyclist in St Peters Park Road standing by his motorcycle preparing to drive off and the police appealed for that person to come forward.

The owner of the yellow Chevette came back at 9.20pm with his brother and they towed the car away. When the men were questioned about the night, they said that in the twenty minutes that it took them to tow the car away, they didn't remember seeing David Short's white Rover car. As such, the police questioned whether David Short had gone out again during that period after having returned at 8.45pm and that if he did, then where?

At about the same time, 9.20pm, about a quarter of a mile away, a witness said that he saw two men shouting in a car. He said that it was an orange or red old-style saloon car and said that the car was driving erratically, stopping and starting. He said that he then saw it stop just around the corner outside the Albion public house and that he saw two men get out from each side and start shouting at each other.

At about 9.45pm, David Short's wife and his mother left the Pleasurama bingo hall in Ramsgate where they had been playing bingo. By the time they got home at 10pm David Short had been murdered. They found his body lying on the pathway between two broken milk bottles and then called for an ambulance.

At about the same time that David Short was shot, a man was seen running off down a nearby alleyway.

When the police described David Short they said that he wasn't very popular and that he had had many threats made to him noting the threat to his life in the Castle Keep two years earlier and the fact that someone had poured paint stripper over his car a month before he was murdered as well as the man that was seen arguing with him at his house. As such the police said that there could have been many reasons for his death but said that they were not clear about what the actual motive was.

However, his wife later claimed that David Short was a Jekyll and Hyde character and that she had spent 15 years of anguish living with him and his lies.

The police noted that CS gas was illegal to sell in the UK, but said that it was possible to buy it in France and they showed pictures of two canisters of such CS gas at an appeal that might have been used in the hope that someone might recognise them as something they remembered someone possessing. The police also noted that a man called the police incident desk shortly after the murder to say that someone had bought some CS gas in Dover for a job in Margate. They police said that the man had promised to call back but never did and appealed for him to call again.

The police noted that the fact that CS gas was used to incapacitate David Short was an important aspect of the case as CS gas was not easy to get hold of.

In the police appeal, they said that they were looking for three sets of people:

1. Man seen at 9.15pm near David Short's house by the motorcycle.
2. Two men in the old-style red saloon car arguing about a quarter of a mile away.
3. The man seen running away through the alleyway at about the time that the ambulance arrived at David Short's house.

In 2001 an anonymous letter was sent to the police claiming to reveal the identity of the murderer. It was a hand-written letter with a Dorset postmark and the police appealed for the writer of the letter to come forward. The police said, 'Officers do think it may provide the key to the inquiry. They do not think it's a crank or some elaborate hoax. We don't know what the motive of the letter was, but in these circumstances there's always a lot of speculation about someone wanting to get something off their chest. But we don't have any firm idea why someone would want to pass on this information now, after 14 years.

The ideal outcome of the inquiry would be if the author of the letter came forward. Otherwise maybe someone else knows something about it'.

A Detective Inspector added, 'The author of this letter clearly has information that is key to this inquiry and we would appeal for that person to come forward and contact us as soon as possible. We can assure their confidentiality'.

David Short's wife, who described David Short as a Jekyll and Hyde character said that she had been working 14-hour days in order to pay off his debts and that one time she had opened her front door to meet a man with a shotgun who had knocked her out of the way and had stormed through the house looking for David Short. She later said that she had discovered that he had remortgaged their house seven times without her knowing and that he had been declared bankrupt twice and had left debts of at least £50,000.

She added that after he died she found fourteen hard-porn videos stashed away under the stairs at their house and said that she had feared that he had been having an affair with another man.

She also said that she had suspected him of drug running after he had made a secret trip to Jersey. She said that after his death she found out that he had even made two trips to Jersey that she didn't know anything about.

She said that as their relationship deteriorated and she became aware of David Short's double life he walked out on her and their 9-year-old child in January 1988 and it was at that time she said that she discovered that the remortgage payments on thier house had fallen behind. She said that the house was then repossessed and that she had to move into a holiday home. She said that it was just before David Short left her that the man with the shotgun had called at their house and stormed in. She said, 'I just froze and let him run through. When someone charges past you with a gun, you don't worry about stopping them. He realised Dave wasn't there and left. Seconds later Dave came in. He must have seen the man leave'.

She claimed that in order to avoid money lenders David Short had started to park around the corner and would peer round the corner to see if the coast was clear.

David Short's wife added that David Short had had at least two official girlfriends whilst they were together, one who was several years older than him, and said that there were also another half a dozen other women that he would see occasionally. She said that on one occasion she went to one of the women's houses and that when she knocked at the door David Short had answered it wearing a dressing gown and said that the woman was standing behind him in a negligee. She said that the thing that amazed her about it was that the woman's house was decorated almost exactly like her house, even down to the same fish tank, noting that the only difference was that her bathroom was bigger.

David Short's wife said, 'Even the women he was with were like me but a few years older. It was like being in a time warp. He was so cool and just asked me if I had come round because their son was ill'.

She said that on another occasion she had answered the phone to be asked whether David Short would be wanting the hotel room with the jacuzzi.

She added, 'They say love is blind. I just held on. People don't get divorced in my family and I was working so hard I didn't have time to think about what was going on. It's only now when I look back that things seem to fit in place. He even took his women to the same places as he took me. One night we were in a nightclub and one of his girlfriends was there. All his friends knew about her and the situation with us and seemed to accept it. I was the only one who did not know'.

She said that when he got beaten up he would deny it and said that on one occasion he had come home with a broken nose and cuts on his body and had told her that he had fallen.

Amrik Singh

Age: 32

Sex: male

Date: 13 Sep 1988

Place: Park Avenue, Southall, Middlesex

Amrik Singh was stabbed through the heart in a brawl.

A 58-year-old priest was tried for his murder but acquitted. He said that Amrik Singh had fallen on his own blade.

The priest was from Banbury Avenue in Stratford-upon-Avon and was described as a religious fanatic.

The brawl was described as a battle between rival factions of a Sikh temple.

It was heard that the priest had been a member of the trust that ran the temple but that there had been a dispute with another faction that wanted control.

The priest said that he was confronted by four men and that Amrik Singh fell on his own blade during the struggle.

John Ward

Age: 24

Sex: male

Date: 12 Sep 1988

Place: The Avenue Pub, Church Road, Manor Park

John Ward was stabbed in the toilet of The Avenue public house after he and his brother were confronted by five men with knives.

He had been stabbed seven times.

An unemployed painter and decorator was tried for his murder but found not guilty. Whilst it wasn't suggested at the trial that he had actually been the man that had stabbed John Ward, it was stated that he had been with the group that had attacked him and as such he was charged with both murder and violent disorder but was acquitted of both charges. The unemployed painter and decorator admitted that he had been drinking in The Avenue public house at the time of the murder but said that he was not involved. He said that he had seen the attackers come out of the lavatory and said that as they came out e also left the pub. He said that he saw four to five men come out and that he didn't want to be involved in any fight and so he put his pint down and left and went home to his mother's place where he lived.

It was noted that the unemployed painter and decorator had been emphatic about his innocence and had told the police when he was first arrested that he had not been a party to the violence. He had told the police that he had seen the men come out of the lavatory but had not seen anyone with any weapons.

John Ward had been attending a wake at the pub following the death of his third child which was still born. After being stabbed he was taken to the same hospital that his third child died at where he died two days later.

He had lived in Altmore Avenue, East Ham.

Lee Boxell

Age: 15

Sex: male

Date: 10 Sep 1988

Place: High Street, Sutton, Surrey

Lee Boxell was last seen on the High Street outside the Tesco supermarket in Sutton at 2.20pm on 10 September 1988.

It was thought that he had been abducted and murdered. In 2012 the police said that there was no evidence that Lee Boxell was alive anymore, either under his own name or any other name.

It was first thought that he had gone missing after going off to a football match, but it was later thought that he had gone to an informal youth club known as The Shed at St Dunstans in Croydon where teenagers would gather to drink and smoke and that his disappearance was connected with some event that happened there.

In 2014 several men were arrested for his murder. Three men aged between 41 and 78 were arrested on suspicion of murder, conspiracy to pervert justice, and indecency with children, but they were all released without charge. A 42-year-old woman was also arrested on suspicion of conspiracy to pervert justice and indecency with children but was similarly released without charge.

It was suggested that he might have been killed after witnessing a sexual assault on another person at The Shed, details of which only came to light in 2012.

When he was last seen he had said that he might go to watch a football match at Selhurst Park in north Croydon between Charlton and Millwall. It was also thought that he might have instead gone to Plough Lane to watch Wimbledon play West Ham or even gone to a local match between Charlton Athletic and Bromley in Colston Avenue, Sutton. However, no one ever came forward to say that they had seen him at any of the games. Further, it was thought that if he had been outside the Tesco supermarket at 2.20pm that he probably wouldn't have had time to have got to any of the matches which would have kicked off at 3pm.

Lee Boxell was described as:

- White.
- 5ft 5in to 5ft 6in tall.
- Slim build.
- Light brown hair.
- Quietly spoken.
- Wearing faded black jeans, a white Flintstones t-shirt and brown suede shoes.

In 2012 a witness came forward to say that Lee Boxell had been at an unofficial youth club in the annexe of St Dunstan's Church in Cheam, which was known locally as 'The Shed'. It was said that the existence of The Shed was previously unknown to the police but that upon further inquiries they determined that there was substance to the claim. The police said that following their investigations they determined that there had been paedophiles operating in the area at the time that Lee Boxell vanished, including a 52-year-old grave digger at the church who was said to have run The Shed. The grave digger was himself convicted of sexually abusing four girls aged 11 to 15 years old that had attended The Shed in 2011 when he was 75 years old and sentenced to 11 years. The grave digger was a former soldier.

It was said that the grave digger would convince the teenagers to have sex with him by convincing them that he had supernatural powers. It was said that he had told the children that he was a warlock and that he could pass on his supernatural powers by having sex with them. At his trial in 2011 it was heard that he would have sex with the children on a tombstone, stating that the girl would get their power from a 'black floating monk' that haunted the church. It was also heard at the grave diggers trial that one girl that he had had sex with had told him that she thought that she was pregnant and said that he had told her that if he had sex with him again that she would no longer be pregnant.

Following the conviction of the grave digger, the police excavated parts of the graveyard but found nothing. The police carried out excavations twice, once between June and September 2012 and then again in April 2013.

Following a later appeal on the television program Crimewatch in 2013, another person came forward to say that they had been abused as a child at The Shed and the police said that they were working on the theory that Lee Boxell had been trying to stop the sexual abuse and that he had been murdered because of that or that he had seen something that had resulted in an incident in which he had lost his life, either intentionally or accidently.

The police said that they thought that The Shed had been targetted by a number of sexual predators because it was a gathering place for teenagers who would go there to drink and smoke. The Shed was described as a dilapidated hut on the church's grounds. The Shed later burned down.

It was thought that Lee Boxell might have gone there after leaving his friend outside Tesco's and the police later said that they thought that he had been murdered there. A detective Inspector said, 'I believe that Lee was assaulted by one person and that they had help from one or more others to dispose of the body and/or cover up the death. I would like to appeal to that young person who was sexually assaulted to come forward. Your evidence would confirm Lee's presence at the shed and help to identify his assailant. I accept and wish to make it clear that it may not have been the intention to kill Lee and that your role in assisting the main attacker will be taken into account. But you have to take responsibility for your actions and face the consequences before it is too late for Lee's family. Someone knows what happened to Lee and where his body is buried'.

The police said that they thought that Lee Boxell had been at the Shed on Saturday 10 September 1988 and that he had seen someone being sexually assaulted and that in the following course of events he was killed and that the person that was sexually assaulted might have been involved in either causing Lee Boxell's death or disposing of his body and appealed for that person to come forward.

It was said that on the morning that he disappeared that he had wanted to see his team Sutton United play, but that they were playing away in Blackpool and that he had instead gone off to Sutton High Street with a friend where they had window shopped. His friend said that when he last saw Lee Boxell at 2.20pm he had told him that he might go to watch Crystal Palace play.

It was noted that there was no CCTV evidence found that covered his movements after he was last seen.

His parents said that they first became worried at about 5pm after he failed to contact them as he normally would have done so.

Lee Boxell had lived in Cheam and was last seen in Sutton High Street which was about a mile away. St Dunstan's Church was closer to his home in Cheam. Selhurst Park, where the football game Lee Boxell said he was going to watch was in Croydon which was about five or six miles away.

It was noted that following his disappearance his parents kept his bedroom exactly as it was when he left including his maths homework that he had left out on his desk.

Lee Boxell had been a pupil at Cheam High School and was an only child.

Wayne Lomas

Age: 31

Sex: male

Date: 30 Aug 1988

Place: Greenbank Road, Southville, Bristol

Wayne Lomas was found in a slab of concrete at a home in Greenbank Road, Bristol in October 1993.

His remains were found in a one ton slab of concrete hidden beneath the floorboards of a terraced house in Greenbank Road in the Southville area of Bristol. The concrete slab was found on 11 October 1993 when the police raided five homes around south Bristol under a warrant for conspiracy to murder. His remains were identified eleven days later on 19 October 1993 after the police chipped away at the concrete block to reveal them.

The owners of the property had been away on holiday in Spain at the time of the discovery but were said to have not been involved with his murder.

Wayne Lomas had been a car dealer and moneylender and was believed to have had criminal connections. It was thought that he had been the victim of a gangland killing and that he had been given a concrete overcoat. The police said that when he first went missing that they thought that he had been kidnapped but later suspected that he had been murdered. The raids in 1993 were carried out after the police reviewed his case following other recent investigations by the regional crime squad into organised crime in the south Bristol area. It was said that top secret electronic equipment had been used in the searches that had resulted in the concrete slab that Wayne Lomas was entombed in being found. It was said that the police had to remove about 18 inches of earth and other debris before they struck the concrete slab.

Wayne Lomas had been single and living in Westleigh Park in Bristol at the time he disappeared on 30 August 1988. He was first noted as being missing after his neighbours found his house unlocked and his pet dogs running loose in the garden and a meal left out prepared on a table inside and his tumble dryer still running.

Four men were questioned over his murder but released without charge.

A builder from Knowle in Bristol was later convicted of perverting the course of justice after it was found that he had helped to dispose of Wayne Lomas's body knowing that he had been murdered and given a two year prison sentence but was released due to the amount of time that he had spent on remand.

Wayne Lomas had previously been acquitted of attempted murder after he was tried at a Crown Court in 1985 for allegedly shooting a man in the neck and face outside a nightclub in Bristol.

He was from Hengrove.

Ray Anstey

Age: 55

Sex: male

Date: 29 Aug 1988

Place: Pennycross Sports and Social Club, Plymouth

Ray Anstey was stabbed to death at the Pennycross Sports and Social Club by robbers on the night of 29 August 1988.

His post mortem examination showed that he had been stabbed several times in the chest with a knife.

He was the steward of the club and was probably locking up for the night when he was ambushed by his murderers.

His body was found in the lavatory the following morning by cleaners where they turned up for work.

It was thought that the robbers had gone there to ransack the fruit machines after closing time which they had emptied.

A witness said that they saw two men at about 12.10am on 30 August 1988 getting into a dark brown estate car, which was thought could possibly have been a Mark 3 Cortina. The police said that they wanted to speak to the two men or anyone else that saw them.

The phone wires at the club had been ripped out.

Ray Anstey's ring, wallet, a bunch of keys and a lighter were also noted as having been missing.

His wallet had contained some membership cards and a photograph of his 8-year-old daughter.

The ring was noted for being unusually large and with having a gem in the corner from which a sunburst effect radiated. The ring was nine-karat gold.

Michael Williams

Age: 43

Sex: male

Date: 27 Aug 1988

Place: Highgate Wood, North London

Michael Williams was found dead in Highgate Wood on the morning of Saturday 27 August 1988.

He had been hit in the throat.

He was last seen on the Friday 26 August 1988 before the August bank holiday weekend. His body was found the following morning 27 August 1988 at about 7.40am in Highgate Wood near to where he lived.

He had gone to a pub in Pimlico where he worked for the Home Office on the Friday afternoon with some work colleagues after which he got the tube home to Highgate.

The following day his credit card was used in a tandoori restaurant in Southgate.

It was thought that the motive was robbery but there was also a possible sexual motive as he was a bisexual.

It was also thought that the person that killed him might have been a karate expert because the force required to cause the damage to his throat was significant and karate experts said that it would take years of experience to be able to cause that much damage.

Michael Williams had lived in Highgate all his life and had been married for 18 years and had a two-year-old daughter. He was also an active member of the local church.

It was heard that he tried to spend as much time with his daughter as he could, and he worked flexi-hours and often came home early to look after her.

Michael Williams had worked for the Home Office in Horseferry house in Pimlico and had helped to set up the Police National Computer.

He had been at work at 6pm on the Friday 26 August 1988 at about 6pm when his wife called him at his work to ask how long he was going to be until he got home and he told her that he was going to work for about another hour and that he expected to be home for about 8pm. It was said that he had been under a lot of pressure at work at the time and that for the previous week he had been staying late each evening to finish a particular project.

However, shortly after a colleague convinced him to go out for drinks with some of the other staff and they went off together to the Paviours Arms in Page Street, Pimlico where they stayed drinking until about 11.15pm. Michael Williams left for home at about 11.15pm with a colleague, taking the same tube together, with his colleague changing trains at Victoria station at about 11.35pm and leaving Michael Williams on the tube train to continue his journey, which was the last time that he was seen alive. It was noted that the Paviours Arms was demolished in 2003.

It was noted that when he had left the office and gone to the Paviours Arms Michael Williams had taken his work things with him in a black and white plastic bag with the initials i-D in white in a black star which was itself in a white circle on a black square.

The plastic bag was known to have contained a black Vodapage radio-pager, a computer manual and his Home Office pass. The bag and contents were all missing when his body was found as was his gold signet ring and a distinctive Rolex watch that he had been wearing. The Rolex watch was noted as having been made for him about 17-years earlier. It was noted for having a peculiar clasp around the face of the watch.

It was thought that from Victoria tube station that Michael Williams had continued on through Green Park and Oxford Circus to Warren Street or Euston where he would have changed onto the Northern line at which time it would have been about 11.45pm. From there he would have got on the train to Highgate, passing through Mornington Crescent, Camden Town, Kentish Town, Tufnell Park, Archway and then on to Highgate.

However, it was noted that it was by no means certain that he did take his usual route home that night and it was thought that he might have met someone on the way.

It was noted that if he had got off at Highgate Station that his walk home would have taken him past Highgate Wood where he was found dead the following morning.

However, it was thought that he might have gone on through to East Finchley and got off there as a ticket collector said that he saw someone that looked like him there at about 12.30am on the Saturday morning 27 August, noting that he had asked him where the toilets where, noting that he told him that they were closed at that time.

Highgate Wood was noted as being a popular spot, even early in the mornings. His body was found by a woman at 7.40am as she walked her dog. He was dead on the ground to the side of a main path through the wood off of Lanchester Road.

He had been killed by a single blow to the throat.

The police said that they didn't know if he was killed there or whether he had been killed elsewhere and his body then dumped there. It was said that several people said that they had used the path even earlier that morning at about 6.05am but had not seen his body. It was said that at about 6.05am a man had walked his dog past the spot where Michael Williams's body was found but said that he didn't see anything. However, he added that his dog had continued along the path and round the corner and that when he followed it he saw that it was barking at a strange man that was standing there motionless and staring into space as if in a trance. He said that his dog, an Alsatian dog, was barking at the man and attacking him, but that the man was not reacting at all and was just standing there motionless with his back to a tree. He said that the man looked as though he was hypnotised and that it was absolutely unreal how he stood there without moving.

The man was described as being about 6ft tall, white, with a slim build, longish brown hair and a beard of the same colour.

At about 6.50am a man was opening the main gates to the wood but said that he didn't see the strange man nor did he see Michael Williams's body.

Another person also said that they had walked along the path at 6.55am and also saw nothing by the path.

As such, the police said that they thought that Michael Williams's body was dumped there between 7am and 7.40am, possibly from a car.

It was further noted that on Sunday 28 August 1988 Michael Williams's credit card was used at the New Arjun Tandoori restaurant at 37 Friern Barnet Road in Southgate, about three miles away from Highgate Wood. The card was a Lloyds Bank Access card. the police said that they wanted to trace whoever had used the card, noting that even if it was only to eliminate them from the murder investigation as they might not have been the person that attacked Michael Williams and might have come into possession of the card through some other means, such as finding it somewhere or buying it.

Whilst the police said that they thought that robbery was the motive, they also said that there was a sexual aspect to the case as Michael Williams was bisexual and they thought that he might have met someone and even left them before he was attacked and they appealed for such a person to come forward.

Elena Dimitri

Age: 20

Sex: female

Date: 14 Aug 1988

Place: Stanway Street, Hoxton, London

Elena Dimitri was stabbed to death in her home.

She had suffered two stab wounds to her neck and a third stab wound just above her left breast.

An unemployed man was tried for her murder but found not guilty.

Her boyfriend, a 21-year-old postman, said that he went to her flat to take her out on a date and that when he let himself in he saw a man standing near her body with a knife who then fled. He later identified the man as the man that was tried, but the man that was tried said that he had been playing tennis with his brother at the time.

Elena Dimitri's boyfriend said that he had seen her about two hours earlier when he had dropped her off at her flat and made plans to pick her up later that evening.

When Elena Dimitri was found she was slumped in a chair with stab wounds. She had been wearing only her underclothes, a boob tube and a dressing gown and it was thought that she had let her murderer into her flat willingly.

Elena Dimitri's boyfriend said that the man that fled the flat was black, about 6ft 2in tall, aged about 25, with a small beard and had been wearing sunglasses. He said that when he went into her flat, he saw the shadow of a man in the hallway standing with his back to the sink and with a knife in his right hand. Elena Dimitri's boyfriend said that he then asked the man why he was there and also asked where Elena Dimitri was and said that the man made some sort of reply and then swung the knife at him. Elena Dimitri's boyfriend said that he then yelled, 'Don't stab me, please don't stab me' and that the man then pushed past him with the knife in his right hand and a small clutch bag in his left hand and ran out of the flat.

Elena Dimitri's boyfriend said that he then ran through Elena Dimitri's flat looking for her an found her slumped in a chair and that he then called for an ambulance, but she was already dead.

It was heard that there was no sign of any forced entry and that nothing in the flat had been stolen. It was also noted that Elena Dimitri had not been sexually assaulted and that there was no sign of a struggle. The trial heard that it was thought that Elena Dimitri had known her murderer and that she had let him in willingly whilst dressed in her dressing gown.

The court heard that Elena Dimitri was a drug user and took heroin. It was also noted that her previous boyfriend and the father of her two-year-old daughter who was himself a heroin addict was in prison at the time of her murder. The police noted that many of her friends were either unable or unwilling to give evidence in the investigation.

The man tried was arrested on 20 October 1988. He had been living with Elena Dimitri's previous boyfriend's sister in her flat in Hackney. When he was searched, he was found to be in possession of a knife that he was said to have taken from Elena

Dimitri's flat after her brother left it there on a previous occasion. When the knife was examined by forensic scientists it was determined that it could have been the knife used to murder Elena Dimitri.

The man admitted knowing Elena Dimitri but denied murdering her.

Samuel Graham Williamson

Age: 58

Sex: male

Date: 10 Aug 1988

Place: Cotlands Road, Lansdowne, Bournemouth, Dorset

Samuel Graham Williamson was killed, and his body set alight in Cotlands Road, Bournemouth, on 10 August 1988.

He had been strangled with a leather belt. He had also been punched and his head hit against some concrete posts in what was described as a frenzied attack. His body had been burnt almost beyond recognition. The police said that he was 'almost unrecognisable' when he was found.

His burnt body was found in the grounds of the DHSS offices in Cotlands Road but it was thought that he had been murdered elsewhere although it was not said where.

The police said that they had been puzzled by the lack of a motive.

The police appealed for help from motorbike enthusiasts that might have been in the Bournemouth area at the time of the murder as well as for anyone who recognised the belt that Samuel Williamson had been strangled with, describing it as a biker's belt. The belt had had a heavy brass buckle. A picture of the belt was released as it was thought to have been hand made and distinctive, but it was later determined that thousands of them had been made around 1980.

The police also appealed for anyone that might have seen a fight in a dark alleyway that was used by local residents as a short cut which was near to where Samuel Williamson had lived in the Lansdowne area.

A man was charged with his murder in 1988, but the case against him was dropped due to lack of evidence.

However, he was charged again in October 2006 but was acquitted by a jury at Winchester Crown Court. He was rearrested in 2005 after the police carried out a cold case review and found his DNA amongst the material found under Samuel Williamson's fingernails.

It was also heard that his fingerprints were on a lager can that was found in the crook of Samuel Williamson's arm and that another lager can had the man's fingerprints as well as one of his hairs on it.

At the time of the man's arrest in 1987 he had been living in Glasgow. The man said that he had had a severe drinking problem at the time Samuel Williamson was murdered and that he remembered little about the events around the murder but said that he was sure that he would have recollected seeing Samuel Williamson murdered or having been involved if he had been.

Samuel Williamson was an Irish bachelor and was born in County Antrim. He was said to have had relations in Bournemouth and Ballymena.

Man

Age: unknown

Sex: male

Date: 10 Aug 1988

Place: Empire Ballroom, Leicester Square, London

It was reported that a man was murdered at the Empire Ballroom in Leicester Square on 10 August 1988, but nothing more is known.

A man was charged with having attempted to pervert the course of justice by blaming the murder of people that he knew to be innocent. It was said that at the Empire Ballroom on 10 August 1988, knowing that a serious arrestable offence had taken place, that he had removed the victim from the scene and attempted to falsely accuse person that he knew to be innocent of the offence.

However, no further information about the murder can be found.

The case is assumed to be a different murder at the Empire Ballroom in Leicester Square to that of Richard Henvey who was stabbed to death there on 2 April 1987 and whose murder is unsolved.

Percy Francis

Age: 71

Sex: male

Date: 2 Aug 1988

Place: 3 Upper Park Avenue, Rushden, Northamptonshire

Percy Francis was found stabbed and hit with an object at his bungalow at 3 Upper Park Avenue, Rushden on Tuesday 2 August 1988.

It was known that Percy Francis was a homosexual and had had hundreds of young men to his bungalow for sex sessions.

It was noted that nothing had been stolen from his bungalow and that there was no sign of a break-in having taken place and it was thought that whoever had been in his home had been there with his permission.

It was also determined that someone had cut his hair in the two days before his murder. It was thought that a certain known youth might have cut his hair, but he was never traced.

Another man that the police said that they were trying to trace was a 26-year-old who it was said had moved to the Midlands in fear after having been attacked twice by Donald Nilsen, the man convicted of six murders and two attempted murders.

The police said that they had traced about 200 people that had visited his bungalow but said that they knew that there were many others who had not been traced.

Gordon Benedict Ware

Age: 18

Sex: male

Date: 22 Jul 1988

Place: Dorking, Surrey

Gordon Benedict Ware was stabbed after in Dorking following a road traffic accident.

A 42-year-old man was tried for his murder but acquitted. It was stated that he had claimed self-defence, but Gordon Ware's case is still listed as unresolved by Surrey police.

Gordon Ware died from a single stab wound shortly after leaving a pub where he had been celebrating a friend's birthday.

Gordon Ware was a mechanic and had lived in Westcott near Dorking.

Diana Maw

Age: 36

Sex: female

Date: 20 Jul 1988

Place: Stanley Court, Woodfield Road, Ealing, West London

Diana Maw was shot with a crossbow on the landing outside her second floor flat in Stanley Court, Woodfield Road in Ealing on Wednesday 20 July 1988.

She had been shot in the back of her head with a six-inch crossbow bolt and had died almost instantly after it severed her spinal cord.

No one heard anything which was partly because there was only one other flat connected to her second-floor landing which was a dead-end. Her flat was on Woodfield Road which was described as busy. There was a school and an old people's home nearby, but no one noticed anything.

Her body was found by her 15-year-old neighbour at 11.30am on 20 July 1988. He said, 'I will always be haunted by what I saw. I keep seeing her lying there with this arrow sticking out of the side of her head'.

She had been wearing a green suit and was found with her briefcase beside her and her lipstick and makeup in her hand.

A 35-year-old woman was charged with her murder but later discharged after Crown Prosecution lawyers said they did not have enough evidence to prosecute. It was said that the evidence against her was circumstantial.

The woman had been a design consultant and had lived in Aynhoe Road in West Kensington.

Diana Maw's handbag had been stolen when she was murdered and it was later found abandoned on a footpath behind her flat about a month later. The police said the finding of her handbag was significant as it indicated the route that her killer might have taken after the murder.

At about the same time an ice cream seller came forward to say that he had seen a man openly carrying a crossbow in the same street. He was described as:

- Aged 19 to 20.
- About 5ft 8in tall.
- Cold hard eyes.

Diana Maw had been due to give a half-day training session on the Wednesday she was murdered and it was said that she had been such a meticulous worker that when she failed to attend the training session her colleagues became immediately concerned.

The crossbow bolt was an aluminium-shafted one with a steel tip which was thought to have been fired from a mini-crossbow. It was said that the mini-crossbow was probably a small one about 12 to 14 inches across that would have been readily concealable in a plastic bag or holdall or even beneath a coat or anorak. The police said that they thought that the crossbow used had been a Barnet Trident, noting that they thought it would have had a 75lb Magnum prod, making it one of the most powerful crossbows available on the market. The police said that the crossbow would have been readily purchased by mail order but also appealed for anyone that had had a crossbow stolen from them to come forward.

However, the police said that the mini-crossbow was not an accurate weapon, adding, 'It is not the sort of weapon that an intelligent man would use if he was planning a cold-blooded murder'.

The design consultant, whose ex-boyfriend Diana Maw had been seeing, was arrested and charged with her murder on 30 November 1988.

The design consultant had been seeing Diana Maw's boyfriend for several years before he left her for Diana Maw and it was said that she had been quite upset over the breakup.

The general timeline of events are:

- February 1988: Diana Maw was said to have started seeing the design consultant's boyfriend.
- May 1988: Diana Maw's boyfriend left the design consultant for Diana Maw.
- 12 June 1988: Diana Maw's briefcase was stolen from outside her flat.
- 20 July 1988: Diana Maw was shot in the head with a crossbow bolt outside her flat.
- August 1988: The police released a photofit of a suspect that they said had been seen with a crossbow two days

before the murder. He was described as being between 19 and 21 years old and about 5ft 8in tall.

- 12 August 1988: Police report that they had narrowed their search down to five or six unidentified suspects.
- 30 November 1988: The design consultant was charged with murder.
- 2 December 1988: The design consultant was refused bail after it was claimed that there was a real risk that she might commit another crime and that three was 'a real fear for the safety of her ex-boyfriend at her hands'. It was also claimed that she might have tried to interfere with witnesses. It was also submitted that the design consultant might attempt to harm herself if given bail.
- 20 April 1990: Crown Prosecution Service offered no evidence at the design consultant's trial and she was acquitted.
- 2am 25 June 1990: A fire broke out at the boyfriend's home in Napier Avenue, Fulham. The police said that a forensic examination showed that inflammable substances had been used in several places to start the fire.
- June 1990: The design consultant was charged with setting fire to her ex-boyfriends' home. However, the arson charge was later dropped.

- November 1990: The design consultant was charged with breaking into her ex-boyfriends' yacht and stealing a diary.
- March 1991: The design consultant was acquitted at a trial on the charge of stealing the diary from the yacht.

Diana Maw had been a recruitment consultant with the Industrial Society earning £25,000 a year and had lived in what was described as a luxury flat in Woodfield Court, Ealing, worth £130,000. The company that she worked for was described as a top head-hunting company.

She had strong ties to Dundee in Scotland.

Diana Maw had been educated at Cheltenham Ladies College, which was described as an exclusive establishment that cost £6,000 a year and she was described as having been a high achiever.

Following her murder, the police said that they first thought that she had been killed by a mugger. However, they later developed the theory that the design consultant had borne a jealous grudge and had been stalking her ex-boyfriend and Diana Maw which had culminated with the murder. It was claimed that the design consultant had become obsessed with Diana Maw after her boyfriend left her for Diana Maw.

In the period before her murder it was said that Diana Maw had been receiving anonymous phone calls which it was claimed at the trial the design consultant had made.

It was claimed that the design consultant had followed Diana Maw and her ex-boyfriend around and that she had once followed them to the theatre.

A few weeks before her murder Diana Maw had had her briefcase stolen from outside her flat and the police said that they were keen to trace it. The briefcase was described as an upmarket black leather briefcase with a grey velour lining and to have contained her personal information including her name and address. The briefcase was said to have cost over £150 and the police appealed for anyone that had come across it to let them know. The combination to the locks on the case was thought to have been 020851, which was a common number she used.

At the time of her murder she had been planning to move into a £325,000 house with her boyfriend.

It was noted that after the breakup of the design consultant and her boyfriend's relationship that the design consultant was convinced to take a two week sailing holiday with friends in Corsica to help her get over her heartbreak, but that she didn't seem to enjoy it and seemed to have other things on her mind.

It was said that during the police investigation into the design consultant the police had taken statements from over 300 people, many of them friends or workmates of the design consultant and that in some cases details had been given concerning her bizarre actions, state of mind and personal relationships which were later submitted as reasons why she should not be given bail after her arrest in November 1988. It was also suggested at the time that she might try to contact some of the witnesses in an attempt to influence them with regard to the evidence that they had given.

When the design consultant was charged, she denied having had any part in the murder. However, she accepted having followed Diana Maw and her ex-boyfriend about, including going to the theatre when they were there and admitted having behaved in 'an undignified and shameful manner', but she said that she had never made any direct approach to either of them nor threatened either of them with violence.

When she was charged her defence said that the single event that had led to her appearance in court was an identification by a single witness who said that they had not seen a woman, but a man and who could not remember the precise date of the alleged sighting.

After she was acquitted at the magistrates hearing her lawyer said that the Crown Prosecution Service dropped the case because of a 'gaping hole in police evidence'. The lawyer said, 'The police only had very thin circumstantial evidence based on he fact that she was the former girlfriend of Diana Maw's boyfriend. In fact, on her own admission she did behave badly by following the couple around after her split with him, but she was guilty of nothing more than being unlucky in love'.

Following the design consultant's acquittal, she was later arrested for setting fire to her boyfriends house in Fulham and also stealing from his yacht but was cleared of all charges. She later claimed that the police were fixated with her.

Diana Maw's murder brought about a national debate on the legality of owning crossbows and a call for their ban. It was said that the Home Office were looking at the various options which included a ban, or setting up a register off crossbow owners, and issuing crossbow certificates, similar to that required for the purchase of firearms. It was reported that MPs had been campaigning for stricter controls since the introduction of the 1987 Crossbow Act under which traders that sold crossbows to people under 17 years of age, which was illegal, could be jailed for up to six months or fined up to £2,000. It was further noted that over 100,000 crossbows were sold in Britain every year and that many of them had aggressive names. It was also noted that the crossbow was capable of firing a bolt at 135mph and with enough force to pass straight through a person's body.

Patrick Morgan

Age: 20

Sex: male

Date: 12 Jul 1988

Place: Weavers Field, Bethnal Green, London

Patrick Morgan was stabbed in Vallance Road, Bethnal Green on 12 July 1988 following a row at a fairground in Weavers Field.

He died from a stab wound to the heart.

An 18-year-old delivery driver was tried for his murder but acquitted after it was heard that it could not be proved that he had caused the lethal blow. A QC said, 'However suspicious a jury may be they can never safely and satisfactorily reject the possibility that the lethal blow was struck by somebody else'.

At the trial it was heard that although a number of people saw the fight, they all from time to time lost sight of Patrick Morgan which meant that they could not rule out that someone else stabbed him.

Patrick Morgan was stabbed twice in the chest during a knife fight following a row on a dodgem car ride at the fairground. After being stabbed he collapsed in a shop doorway near the fairground.

It was heard that Patrick Morgan had lost his temper after the youth had rammed the stationary dodgem car that he had been standing up in at the time causing him to hurt his head and that he had become angry and then stabbed the youth several times in response. It was heard however that the wounds, which had drawn blood, were not deep and that the youth had then asked his friends whether any of them had a knife and that he was then given a butterfly knife by a 19-year-old computer operator.

It was said that when they next met, Patrick Morgan had a metal cosh as well as the knife and he and the youth who then had the butterfly knife squared up to each other and then left Weavers Field and went into Vallance Road where they started fighting.

It was said that Patrick Morgan had hit the youth over the head with his cosh and that the youth was seen to lunge at Patrick Morgan twice at close range, causing Patrick Morgan to clutch his chest.

At the trial the youth admitted lunging at Patrick Morgan once and said that he didn't mean to kill him. He said, 'I lunged at him twice, but I thought I only got him once. I did not intend to kill him. I was shocked when I was told he had died and I didn't believe the police'. He also said that when he was told that Patrick Morgan had died that he had broken down and cried and that he had since suffered nightmares.

However, he was acquitted at the direction of the judge.

Patrick Morgan had lived in Fernhead Road in Paddington.

Rodney Lockwood

Age: 29

Sex: male

Date: 7 Jul 1988

Place: 126 Kingsland High Street, Hackney, London

Rodney Lockwood died in a fire at 126 Kingsland High Street.

He died from asphyxiation due to smoke inhalation whilst trying to escape. The fire had also completely gutted the building.

It case was known as the Cludo Killing because only one of seven people could have done it.

A 34-year-old warehouse packer was tried for manslaughter at the Old Bailey but acquitted.

When the prosecution presented their case to the jury, they told them that they would have to solve the puzzle by a process of elimination, as in the game of Cluedo. They added, 'It is like a game of Cluedo. You will hear evidence from one of the seven people involved. Then you will have to make up your minds whether or not they had anything to do with it'.

The fire had started at 126 Kingsland High Street, a clothing store, in the early hours. There were several flats above the shop.

There was no sign of a break in and as such it was said that the only people that could have been responsible were the keyholders to the building.

Rodney Lockwood had been a tenant on the top floor of the building.

The warehouse packer had lived on the second floor. He had been rescued from the fire by the police and another man that had lived in the flats.

The man and woman that owned the shop lived elsewhere, but it was said that they had suffered the most in the fire because their entire stock had gone up and they were not insured.

The three other suspects were all tenants that had lived in the flats above the shop.

The warehouse packer became a suspect after he was found to have lied to the police about certain things. It was heard that he had said that his bedroom door had been shut at the time of the fire, but it was later shown that there was scientific proof to show that it was open. It was also heard that the warehouse packer had been seen near the shop by three youths shortly before the fire broke out, but he denied being out.

In his statement he said that earlier in the day he had been out drinking in a pub and playing pool. He then said, 'I went home in the afternoon after buying a bottle of whisky and watched some television and slept'. He said that when he woke up later in the afternoon he went back out to the pub and then later went back home to watch the television programme 'Cats Eyes'. He said, 'I got everything ready to watch the television but then I fell asleep. I remember waking up to go to the toilet and my head was in smoke when I stood up. I thought about smashing the window because it was hard to breathe and all I could hear outside was shouting, shouting, shouting. People were yelling for the keys to get in. I shouted to the people outside that there was an old boy living downstairs, and then I went back to see if I could try and help him'.

The court heard that shortly after the warehouse packer and another person were overcome by smoke and that it was only through the bravery of two policemen that had been on foot patrol at the time and who had noticed the fire that they were saved. They had backed a police van onto the pavement and then put a ladder on top of it and climbed up to get in and rescue the warehouse packer.

The seven people that the prosecution said were the only possible suspects as they were the only people with keys were:

1. The warehouse packer who lived on second floor.
2. Man who lived in flats.
3. Husband who had been asleep elsewhere with his wife but who lost all their uninsured stock.
4. Wife who had been asleep elsewhere with her husband but who lost all their uninsured stock.
5. Tennant.

6. Tennant.
7. Tennant.

Brian Hayward

Age: 51

Sex: male

Date: 4 Jul 1988

Place: Burwood Place, Marble Arch, London

Brian Hayward was shot in the head at near point blank range in Marble Arch on 4 July 1988.

The bullet had gone straight through his head and it was said that he had been dead before he hit the ground.

A 26-year-old surveyor who worked for him was tried for his murder but acquitted. After the surveyor was acquitted the police said that they were not looking for anyone else and had closed their investigation.

The jury took 45 minutes to return their unanimous not guilty verdict.

Brian Hayward was shot with a Luger pistol in an underground carpark in Marble Arch after leaving work.

He was the head of the surveyor's department at Chestertons Estate Agency on Seymour Street, Marble Arch, a company described as being internationally famous and the surveyor reported to him.

He usually left his office at about 6.45pm and arrived home around 8pm and was described as a creature of habit.

He drove a company BMW which was kept in a high security underground car park in Marble Arch that required a plastic entry card to gain access to.

A shot was heard at about 7pm and the police arrived within 10 minutes. It was said that the police thought that his murder had appeared so professional that they first thought that he had been the victim of an underworld execution or an act of terrorism.

However, it was said that the police could find no reason why anyone would want to murder him, describing him as a man without enemies. He had been happily married for 27 years and had two grown up children, aged 24 and 23 and at the time of his murder he had been studying for a degree in law at Guildford University.

He had worked for Chestertons Estate Agency for 35 years and had been a partner with the firm since 1973.

However, when the police asked for a statement from all of the staff in Brian Hayward's department, they found that the surveyor acted strangely and asked to speak to a solicitor before he gave an account of his movements. It was heard that when he did make his statement, he said that he had been opening up a gym at 7pm where he was having a karate class and that he had never had any problems with Brian Hayward. However, it was later determined that the time he had given was wrong and that he had been reprimanded by Brian Hayward previously three times.

It was heard that Brian Hayward had threatened to dismiss the surveyor two weeks before he was murdered. It was said that he had reprimanded the surveyor in writing three times in the previous five months and had added in his last letter, 'Further failure in this respect will provide grounds for dismissal'.

The three warnings were:

1. Using company notepaper for private matters.
2. Verbally and physically abusing a woman member of staff.
3. Sub-standard work.

It was also heard that the other members at the karate class at the gym denied that the surveyor had been there by 7pm and that one of them said that the surveyor had reminded him not to forget his alibi, adding, 'It can mean 10 or 15 years to me'.

Following their investigation, the police developed the theory that the surveyor had shot Brian Hayward because he was holding his career back.

The surveyor had been a former Territorial Army paratrooper. It was said that whilst he appeared to have a successful yuppy style job, that he actually lived at home with his mother in a terraced house in Peckham and that many of his friends were criminals and that he had had a luger pistol and a sawn-off shotgun in his bedroom and worked part time as a bouncer and was a loner

When the police spoke to a number of his friends, one of them told them that the surveyor had admitted murdering Brian Hayward, and another said that he had shown them the Luger pistol and let him fire it.

However, at the trial, the surveyor said that he had been set up and that two of his friends had given perjured evidence against him in order to claim the £25,000 reward money. He described them as being 'money grabbing opportunists'. He said that the five prosecution witnesses that gave evidence against him had plotted to put him behind bars for a crime he did not commit.

He said that at the time Brian Hayward was shot that he had been travelling home from work.

At the trial the surveyor had admitted that he was ambitious and had used positive thinking techniques. It was heard that he had written down his life goals on cards that he carried about with him. Goals included:

- A valuable town house.
- A furnished flat.
- A sports car.
- Becoming a Freemason.

- Becoming a Chartered Surveyor.

It was further heard that on other cards, he had detailed aspects of his character that he wanted to assert and that one of the cards had read, 'I am highly ambitious, naturally political, totally ruthless and a winner'.

The court also heard that four of the surveyor's friend said that the surveyor had owned a handgun with three of them saying that it was a Luger, which the prosecution said was the type of gun that had been used to shoot Brian Hayward.

It was also heard at the trial that one of the surveyor's friends had said that he had driven the surveyor to Tower Bridge where he had thrown the Luger into the River Thames.

The court also heard from another one of the surveyor's friends, a man that had once worked as a nightclub doorman with him, who said that the surveyor had taken him to a park once late at night and had handed him the Luger pistol and let him fire it.

Another of his friends said that following the murder, the surveyor had stored the Luger pistol in his garage for a while.

Another of his friends even said that the surveyor had admitted to shooting Brian Hayward to him.

However, after hearing the evidence of some of the surveyor's friends, the judge warned the jury to be careful when considering their statements, noting that one of them had three previous convictions and another had two convictions.

When the prosecution noted that Brian Hayward had threatened to sack the surveyor for misconduct, the surveyor said that it was ridiculous to suggest that he had any reason to murder Brian Hayward. He said, 'I admired and respected Mr Hayward. He was very good at his job. I liked him. He was hard but fair. Mr Hayward was right to reprimand me. I knew I had done wrong and I was over apologetic. I didn't consider this a real problem'.

It was heard that when the surveyor heard that Brian Hayward had been murdered that he had said that he was stunned. He said, 'I remember sitting down and trying to take it all in. I couldn't believe it'.

It was claimed at the trial that he had lied about the time that he had arrived at the gym on the evening of the murder, but the surveyor said that that was not true and that he had simply been mistaken.

The prosecution also claimed that the surveyor had thrown his Barbour jacket, which he had been wearing on the day of the murder, and the gun into the River Thames, but the surveyor said that he had lost it on a train on the day after Brian Hayward was shot.

The prosecution also claimed that the surveyor had had a fascination with guns, but he said that he found them boring.

Whilst he was being cross-examined, the prosecution said, 'You are a highly intelligent and skilful liar. You make things up as you go along', to which the surveyor replied, 'I am not a liar'.

It was noted that the surveyor had graduated top of his year at the Thames Polytechnic.

Louise Kay

Age: 18

Sex: female

Date: 24 Jun 1988

Place: Polegate, Eastbourne, East Sussex

Louise Kay vanished without a trace in the early hours of Friday 24 June 1988.

Neither she nor the car she had been driving, Registration RFG 740R, were ever seen again.

She had been living at home with her parents in Polegate, Eastbourne at the time. She had tried a few jobs but had been unemployed for the month prior to her disappearing and had been planning on going to Cornwall the following week.

On the Thursday night before she vanished, 23 June 1988, she had gone with her boyfriend and some friends to a disco on the pier in Eastbourne. However, on the way back whilst driving in her car home shortly before 4am, with her friend and their boyfriends, Louise Kay had an argument with her boyfriend after he told her that he was unable to go to Cornwall that weekend because of his Giro payment and having to pay the rent on his flat.

Louise Kay's friend said that by the time they got back to her home in Watts Lane, Eastbourne, at about 4am, Louise Kay was calmer but still in a bad mood. It was a four-mile journey home from Louise Kay's friends' home to her own, but she never arrived home. Her friend later said that Louise Kay had told her that she wanted to sleep the night at Beachy Head, and it was thought that she had driven off in that direction.

Louise Kay was 5ft 6in tall, had a slim build, light-brown hair and green eyes.

Her car was a gold Ford Fiesta and had a white driver's side front door. The police asked scrap dealers to check their records for June and July 1988 for any such cars that they might have scrapped.

A convicted serial killer that had been living near Eastbourne at the time was questioned over her disappearance in 2010 but no evidence was found to connect him to her case.

Marie Wilkes

Age: 22

Sex: female

Date: 18 Jun 1988

Place: M50, Bushley, Strensham, Hereford and Worcester

Marie Wilkes was murdered on the M50 whilst making an emergency call to the police after her Morris Marina Coupe car overheated and broke down on Saturday 18 June 1988.

Her jaw had been broken and she had been stabbed in the right side of the neck, severing her carotid artery. Her body was found three miles further along the road from where her car had broken down.

She had been dressed in a pink and white maternity dress at the time with white shoes.

A 32-year-old man was initially convicted of her murder on 10 October 1988 but his conviction was later overturned at a court of appeal five years later in May 1994. His conviction was found to have been unsafe after it was heard that evidence had been kept from his trial. He had maintained his innocence throughout. The 32-year-old man had previously been in the Welsh Guards.

He had been sentenced to a minimum of 25-years in prison.

Following his acquittal, he was awarded damages which were said to have been more than £600,000. The man later died in May 2018.

Marie Wilkes had been 7 and a half months pregnant at the time. She had broken down on the M50 and had gone off to use an emergency telephone leaving her 13-month-old son and 11-year-old sister in her car.

She had been driving to her parents' home in Worcester at the time after visiting her husband at an army cadet camp in Symonds Yat in the Wye Valley where he was an instructor and had been instructing 43 cadets in the Hereford and Worcester Army Cadet Force.

Marie Wilkes had only just passed her driving test two months earlier and it was said that the journey was her first big trip and that she had had no intention of using the motorways and had stuck to the country roads, but it was thought that she had become lost on the way home and had no alternative but to use the M50.

She had left Symonds Yat at 7pm and broke down on the M50 sometime between then and 7.37pm when she made a call from the emergency telephone box which was about 700 yards away from where she had broken down. The emergency phone was number 2076B.

After breaking down on the motorway she walked a short distance to the emergency phone box where she called the West Mercia police at 7.37pm to whom she explained her situation. It was heard that the police had put Marie Wilkes on hold while they contacted her family. However, Marie Wilkes's family told the police at 7.40pm that the only other car they had was being used by Marie Wilkes's father who had gone off on a fishing trip and who could not be contacted. After finding out that Marie Wilkes's family were not able to drive out to assist Marie Wilkes the police attempted to re-open the line with Marie Wilkes at 7.41pm but she was not there and they could only hear the sound of cars driving by along the M50.

The police tried to call the emergency phone at 7.44pm again but got no reply.

Shortly after the second call, a police car that had been driving along the motorway from Strenchsham Service Station at 7.49pm saw Marie Wilkes's 11-year-old sister walking along the hard shoulder of the M50 carrying Marie Wilkes's baby and looking for her.

At about the same time the police contacted a breakdown service and asked them to attend Marie Wilkes's car as soon as possible.

It was thought that during the time that Marie Wilkes's sister had been walking along the hard shoulder that about 200 cars would have passed them, but none of them stopped to help. However, it was said that an unknown man had spoken to Marie Wilkes's 11-year-old sister as she was sitting in the car waiting for Marie Wilkes and it was thought possible that the man had been Marie Wilkes's murderer.

After the police in the patrol car found Marie Wilkes's 11-year-old sister and her daughter at 7.59pm, they put out a radio message stating that Marie Wilkes was missing.

Marie Wilkes's mother then gave the police a description of Marie Wilkes at 8.01pm and four police squad cars were dispatched to the scene.

When the police made further checks, all they found was Marie Wilkes's Morris Marina car abandoned and the emergency phone dangling from its cord.

A police helicopter was sent soon after at 8.10pm, to search the surrounding area with thermal imaging cameras. However, it was noted that because the weather had been hot that day, they found nothing.

The police spoke to Marie Wilkes's mother again at 8.20pm and determined that Marie Wilkes had still not contacted her, and the police then searched the area on foot using 50 policemen and tracker dogs but again found nothing.

At about dawn on the following day 19 June 1988 the police then found blood on and around the emergency telephone that Marie Wilkes had used.

Marie Wilkes's body was found the following day on Monday 20 June 1988 on the side of the motorway about three miles on from where her car had broken down near Strenchsham, partially covered by undergrowth down the side of a steep embankment. The police found evidence to indicate that a car had recently reversed behind the crash barrier nearby which it was thought had be done by her murderer in an effort to hide himself from other traffic as he disposed of her body. The police also found a 20-foot tyre mark on the road above that point.

Her jaw had been broken and it was thought that she had been kicked in the side of her head and she had been stabbed in the neck.

Following the murder the police made an appeal to the public and a person came forward to say that they had seen a man near the scene of the crime on the Saturday evening and the police then released an artist's impression of the man the person had seen.

The man was described as, 'white, with thin, sharp features, a pronounced chin and a long nose, in his 20s, of a youngish appearance. His hair was cut in the modern style, blonde, short and spiky, with possible yellow or orange highlights. He was of smart casual appearance, as if on his way to a night out. He was wearing a blue/white striped shirt, dark or royal blue trousers'.

Following the release of the artists impression, the 32-year-old man was arrested at 7pm on Saturday 25 June 1988 after a work colleague said that the artist's impression was him. The 32-year-old man was a doorman and had been working at a social club in Pentre in South Wales. It was noted that the man had also based his belief that the artist's impression was that of the 32-year-old man as he knew him as a violent man with a criminal history and that he knew he owned a butterfly-knife which he thought might have been the murder weapon.

He was charged with Marie Wilkes's murder on Wednesday 29 June 1988.

It was said that the man had received a £25,000 reward for his information following the 32-year-old man's conviction, although he denied that. However, it was also said that in September 1999, after the 32-year-old man had been released, that he attacked the 32-year-old man at his home with an iron bar, claiming that he had confessed to him.

When the police looked into the 32-year-old man they found that he had had an argument with his pregnant wife at their home in Cwmparc in the Rhondda Valley on the evening of Saturday 18 June 1988 at 6.40pm and that shortly after he had driven to Scotland, which would have taken him along the M50 at about the time that Marie Wilkes was murdered as he headed towards the M6 for the north. However, when the 32-year-old man was charged with Marie Wilkes's murder, he denied it and said that he had taken a different route to the M6 north, taking the Severn Bridge and then taking the M5. However, it was claimed that the route he said he had taken was not the natural choice as it would have added 30 miles to his journey and that he was lying.

Further, the police said that it was not possible for the 32-year-old man to have taken the route that he said he took as they checked the CCTV footage at the Severn

Bridge for the evening of the murder and found no evidence that he had crossed.

When the police examined the 32-year-old man's car they found that one of his tyres had a bold patch which the police said raised their suspicions because of the marks they had found at the scene of the murder.

It was noted that whilst there were traces of blood on the call box that Marie Wilkes had used, there was no blood found in the man's car. It was submitted that if he had attacked her first at the call box, resulting in the blood being found there, and had then driven her to where she was later found that blood would have been found in his car. It was said that at his trial that it had been accepted that the 32-year-old man had stabbed Marie Wilkes at the emergency phone kiosk and had then driven her three miles along the motorway where he had then dumped her body.

However, the 32-year-old man was convicted at Shrewsbury Crown Court on 10 October 1988.

The 32-year-old man appealed his conviction in May 1991, but his appeal was refused after the video footage of the Severn

Bridge crossings was considered which did not show him having crossed it.

However, it was noted that in 1992 another video tape was released detailing a police officer who had seen a car on the hard shoulder undergoing hypnosis which resulted in an investigation by the Police Complaints Commission and the case being reopened.

It was heard that before the 32-year-old man was arrested that the police officer had said that he had seen a silvery-grey Renault car pull up onto the east-bound hard shoulder of the M50 on the evening of the murder, Saturday 18 June 1988 but had not mentioned anything about seeing the letter C in the registration. However, it was noted that his memory of the event went no further than that and so it was decided to put him under hypnosis in the hope that he would recall more and the hypnosis was video-taped. The hypnosis took place four days before the 32-year-old man was arrested. During the hypnosis the policeman gave additional details of the car, stating that he had seen a silvery-grey, non-metallic, non-hatch-back Renault car with chrome bumpers and the registration number C856 HFK. However, it was noted that the 32-

year-old man's car had been a hatch-back Renault with plastic bumpers and had had the registration number C754 VAD. As such, it was stated that there were therefore some damaging inconsistencies in the evidence, which combined with the fact that the video-tape had not been made available to the defence meant that if the jury had seen the evidence that they might have returned a different verdict.

It was noted that the policeman also changed his evidence at the trial and described the number plate that he recollected as being similar to that of the 32-year-old man's car.

It was also noted that the police had failed to make another witness statement available to the court in which the witness said that they had also seen the car pulled over on the M50 but had made no reference to the C-registration. However, before the trial, the same witness made another statement in which they said that they had seen the letter 'C' in the registration, which it was later claimed had been encouraged by the police to help secure the conviction.

It was also later heard in October 1992 that a forensic scientist that had carried out analysis of the 32-year-old man's car had concluded that it was unlikely that Marie Wilkes had ever been in his car. He said that considering the nature of her neck wound that he would have imagined Marie Wilkes to have bled significantly and that even with a thorough sponging, he would not have imagined that no trace would be found on the car's interior fabric when chemical tests were applied if there had been blood there as it was reasonable to suspect. He said, 'Fabric car seats, even if thoroughly sponged, I would expect them to still give only a weak, but a chemical reaction, indicating the presence of blood'.

The investigation into the 32-year-old man's conviction also showed that the police had failed to act on nearly 3000 messages that the original murder inquiry team had received.

It was claimed that the two items of evidence, the hypnosis and first witness statement had been deliberately kept from the trial by the police. Again, it was stated that if the jury had seen the previous statement and been made aware of the inconsistency in describing the car has have a C in the registration, along with the video tape of the policeman that had undergone hypnosis, that they might have returned a different verdict and so that 32-year-old man's conviction was found to be unsafe and was quashed.

When the 32-year-old man was released he described the police as a 'bunch of bastards' and said that they had known four days before his arrest that he was not the murderer.

After the 32-year-old man was released, disciplinary action was taken against the police superintended responsible for the investigation for neglect of duty.

In September 1999 the man that was said to have brought the 32-year-old man to the attention of the police attacked the 32-year-old man at his home in Rhondda with an iron bar. It was said that during the attack he had said to the 32-year-old man, 'You admitted to me the night before you were taken in that you murdered that girl'. The attack was witnessed by the 32-year-old man's wife. However, the man said that he had been acting in self-defence and was not convicted for the assault. It was also reported that the man had said that the 32-year-old man had told him that he had wanted to set fire to the car that he had been driving shortly after the murder.

When the police described her murder, they said, 'It appears to be a totally opportunistic incident'.

Marie Wilkes had been a nurse and was married with a child.

Noel Smith

Age: 40

Sex: male

Date: 1 Jun 1988

Place: Limehouse, East London

Noel Smith was murdered in Limehouse, East London in June 1988.

He was a taxi driver and it was suggested that there was a maniac knifeman with a grudge against taxi drivers killing them after John Landa was murdered in Nottingham in 1982, Sarfraz Ahmed was murdered in Peterborough on Tuesday 15 November 1988 and Derek Brann was murdered on 6 November 1988.

However, nothing more is known about his murder.

Brian Kerr

Age: 30

Sex: male

Date: 14 May 1988

Place: Moncur Street, Calton, Glasgow

Brian Kerr was murdered in Moncur Street, Glasgow.

The police said that they were trying to trace a taxi driver that had taken four men from a public house in Duke Street to the Moncur Street address at about 1.30am where there was an incident about 15 minutes later resulting in Brian Kerr's death. However, nothing more is known about the four men.

Following the incident Brian Kerr was taken to the Royal Infirmary where he died shortly after arriving.

He had lived in Millerfield Place, Glasgow.

Jason Clear

Age: 6

Sex: male

Date: 11 May 1988

Place: Chichester Harbour, Chichester, West Sussex

Jason Clear went missing in Chichester on the evening of Wednesday 11 May 1988 and was later found drowned in the sea.

An extensive search was made for him around Chichester and Sussex and it was reported on 13 May 1988 that his father thought that he had been abducted.

A huge search was carried out involving police frogmen, dog teams, a helicopter and numerous volunteers.

However, Jason Clear was found in the sea on Monday 16 May 1988 after it was trawled up by the crew of the fishing boat Persevere close to the entrance of Chichester Harbour.

He had been out with his family and friends to Itchenor, described as a tiny yachting village on the edge of Chichester harbour, where they had gone out in a boat. However, when they got back, they had had an argument because Jason Clear had wanted to stay in the boat.

It was said that he then went to a public toilet adjoining the harbour master's office and was last seen walking up a nearby path.

He and his family had lived in Gilmore Road in Chichester.

The police said that foul play was not suspected. His post mortem showed that he died from drowning.

Alicia Lamothe

Age: 26

Sex: female

Date: 8 May 1988

Place: Cork Street, London, W1

Alicia Lamothe was killed in a robbery at an office in Cork Street, W1 on 8 May 1988.

Alicia Lamothe was a cleaner and she was murdered after she had turned up to work at the office to do some cleaning and had surprised a gang of burglars.

They strangled and battered her over the head with a fire extinguisher and then set the offices on fire to destroy any forensic evidence.

The gang stole £500 before leaving.

A 17-year-old youth was arrested and during his interview he gave the police the name of the person that he said had beaten and strangled Alicia Lamothe, but he later refused to testify against any of the other people in court and kept a vow of silence which meant that the Crown had to drop their case.

It was said that without the evidence of the 17-year-old that the police did not have enough evidence to convict the prime suspect whose name they had.

Alicia Lamothe was a Filipino and had lived in Leconfield Road in Highbury. She had been married for one week.

At the trial the Crown said that there were no eye witnesses to the murder, no forensic evidence regarding who had been involved and especially no evidence regarding who had been responsible for the murder other than the 17-year-old youth's statement.

The 17-year-old had admitted being at the burglary but said that he had had nothing to do with Alicia Lamothe's murder.

After the situation was detailed before the judge, he said, 'I have come to the conclusion if the prosecution case against the youth was tried I would accede to a submission that there was an insufficient case to answer and direct a not guilty verdict'.

The youth admitted a charge of burglary.

Another 15-year-old youth had been a look out, but his case was adjourned.

It was noted that both the 17-year-old and 15-year-old youths had long records for robbery and dishonesty.

Joan Macan

Age: 81

Sex: female

Date: 6 May 1988

Place: Timbray, Ashbridge Estate, Hertfordshire

Joan Macan was hacked to death outside her home on her 81st birthday after disturbing intruders in the early hours of Friday 6 May 1988.

She was a well-known dog breeder and had judged at many shows including Crufts.

She had lived in Timbray on the Ashbridge Estate in Hertfordshire.

She was seen by her kennel-man earlier in the morning at about 8am on 5 May 1988. After that she went into town for a regular appointment at a hairdresser at 9am. It was noted that she had been going there every Thursday morning for about twelve years.

She was back home by 2pm at which time she met an old friend at her cottage who was also a dog breeder and they talked about using one of Joan Macan's dogs for breeding.

It was noted that Joan Macan was renowned for her Labrador dogs and that people from all round the country would come by and visit her and so it was noted that any number of people could have got a good look at her house.

It was said that by about 6.45pm she was getting ready to go to a meeting of the Kent, Sussex and Surrey Labrador Association, having been made president of the association fifteen months earlier. She was seen to drive off alone by her housekeeper, who lived 100 yards up the road from Joan Macan.

Joan Macan was next seen at the meeting which took place at the The Bell Inn public house in Constan, Surrey, 60 miles away, at about 9.40pm. It was noted as being a long way for Joan Macan to drive, but said that she would always make a special effort to attend the meetings and that it had taken her three hours to get there.

It was noted that at about the same time, 9.40pm, Joan Macan's housekeeper had gone down to Joan Macan's cottage, Timbray, to lock up for the night. The housekeeper said that she knew that Joan Macan disliked coming back to a dark house because of its isolation and so she closed the windows and drew the curtains but left the lights on to make the cottage look occupied before locking up.

The meeting ot the Kent, Sussex and Surrey Labrador Association ended at 11pm and Joan Macan drove home, accompanied in part by another member of the Kent, Sussex and Surrey Labrador Association who drove along with her in his car to the M25 as Joan Macan was said to have been slightly apprehensive about making the journey home at that time in the dark. It was noted that the other member was as such the last person to see Joan Macan alive.

It was heard that a couple that had been courting in a car that was parked up in the lane on the Ashbridge Estate that led to Joan Macan's cottage at about midnight saw a car drive up and down the lane about six or seven times. They said that they didn't notice what make of car it was, but said that they did think that it was a dark four-door saloon. The couple said that they next saw an estate car drive down the track at about 1am which was thought to have been Joan Macan arriving home.

It was thought that Joan Macan was then murdered as she went from her car to her cottage.

Shortly after, the couple that had been in the car in the lane at about 1.30am said they saw an estate car, thought to have been a Bluebird, leaving the cottage along the lane. The police said that they thought that the car had been used by the burglar, but said that they could not rule out the possibility that it was owned by another courting couple in the area and asked for any courting couples that might have been in the area in an estate car to come forward.

The police noted that it was a senseless murder as the burglar could have easily escaped from her cottage when she had arrived and run off into the nearby woods with no problem at all.

The police said that a number of items were stolen in the burglary that they thought would be key to solving the murder, including:

- Bronze antique statue of a pointer dog with a rabbit in its mouth which was signed PJ Manay which was valued at about £2,500.
- Statue bronze of a greyhound with E Fremiet inscribed on the base.
- Bronze statue of a pointer dog on a tree stump over a rabbit. The statue was described as so rare that a copy could not be made but an artist's depiction was drawn up. It was also noted that the rabbit on the base had become detached.

It was also noted that a number of snuff boxes and small ornaments were also taken from her cottage.

The police appealed for all antique and secondhand dealers to contact them if they came across any of the distinctive dog bronze statues that were stolen.

When her will was later heard she had left £1,051,723 gross, £1,030,204 net. She also left £125,000 to the 19th May 1961 charity as well as sharing £75,000 between three other charities, the Royal Vetinary College Animal Care Trust, the Animal Health Trust and the Distressed Gentlefolk's Aid Association. She also left her housekeeper and kennel-man £25,000 each.

Joan Macan was also noted for her work during the second World War during which she had lived in France under a false name and had helped over 80 Allied airmen to escape across enemy lines.

John Lewis

Age: 66

Sex: male

Date: 28 Apr 1988

Place: Bermondsey, London

John Lewis was kicked repeatedly after going to sleep on a bench on 7 August 1987. The assault put him into a coma from which he died nine-months later on 28 April 1988.

A 25-year-old labourer was tried for his murder on the basis of the type of boots he was wearing but the evidence fell apart in court and the judge instructed the jury to acquit him. He had maintained his innocence throughout.

John Lewis was known as John 'Scouse' Lewis and was described as a pint-sized pensioner, being only 5ft 4in tall.

It was heard that the person that had kicked John Lewis had left footprints in blood at the

scene and then fled but returned to offer
John Lewis help.

The police later tracked down the labourer
and arrested him on the grounds that he was
seen to have been wearing working boots
with a chevron sole and steel toe caps. The
police said that there was only one boot sold
in England with a chevron sole and a steel
toe cap which suggested to them that he was
the man that had assaulted John Lewis.

However, it was heard that witnesses gave
conflicting evidence regarding the type of
boots that the labourer had been wearing.

John Lewis had been working as a cleaner at
the time at a printing firm and had just
finished work after which he went to The
George public house where he met some
friends and had between seven and eight
pints.

It was said that after leaving the pub he went
to sleep on a park bench near the pub. A
family that were later walking down an alley
near the pub at about midnight said that they
saw a man holding onto a pillar in the alley
and kicking at something violently.

It was said that the man then disappeared, probably because he had been seen, and that several other people then came over to assist John Lewis who was found lying injured. One of the people that had seen the man kicking at something said that shortly after he went over to help John Lewis the man that he had seen kicking something came back and offered to call an ambulance for John Lewis.

The witness said that the man had been wearing working boots with chevron soles and steel capped toes, noting that the leather was ripped over one of the toes. It was said that other witnesses also noticed the metal shining through his boots.

Another witness said that they also saw quite a bit of blood on his boots.

It was also heard at the trial that the person that had carried out the kicking had left a trail of bloody footprints along the path. The court heard that the footprints were in blood which revealed that the attacker had been wearing boots with a chevron patterned sole.

The labourer had lived in Evelyn Street in Deptford and he was arrested on 17 April 1988. However, when the police went to his home they found no trace of a pair of boots with a chevron sole there. He then told the police that on the night of the murder he had been wearing black working boots.

However, at the trial, a businessman that had seen the labourer on the night of the murder said that he recalled him as having been wearing high or long boots, whilst his son, who had been with him, said that the labourer had been wearing black working boots.

Another witness said that the labourer had been wearing cherry red boots that reached four to six inches above his ankle.

After the judge heard the evidence regarding the boots, the judge said, 'You have a flat contradiction in the prosecution case. The defence takes the view that it would be totally unsatisfactory for any jury to consider convicting this man of murder. On my direction I am going to ask the foreman of the jury to find this man not guilty of all three charges he faces'. The labourer had been charged with murder, attempted murder and causing him grievous bodily harm with intent.

The labourer had denied murdering John Lewis and said that he had been working on a building site during the day and that later in the evening he had visited two pubs and that after he left the second pub at 11pm he wandered around for a while before stumbling on John Lewis after he had been attacked along with the other people.

Abdur Rashid

Age: 46

Sex: male

Date: 27 Apr 1988

Place: Epping Forest, Essex

Abdur Rashid was found dead in Epping Forest, Essex on 27 April 1988. He had been murdered and set on fire.

He was murdered during the Muslim festival of Ramadam which began in April 1988

He was found by some school children that had been following a nature trail.

His body had been wrapped up in a bedspread, tied up with a sash cord and burnt. It was noted that certain parts of the Whitechapel area were being redeveloped and it was thought that the sash cord might have been taken from a local building site where the material was commonly being used and easily obtained.

He was a Bangladeshi Muslim teacher and was well known in the East London area. He had arrived in the United Kingdom in 1979 and had worked part time in the mosque.

It was thought that he was murdered in the East End of London before being taken to Epping Forest and set on fire. It was noted that for Muslims, the burning of a body was the ultimate disgrace.

Abdur Rashid had lived in the Whitechapel district of the East End of London which was said to have contained a tightly knit Bangladeshi community that was centred around the East London Mosque.

It was thought that he had been murdered by a sharp knife such as a dar, which was often used to peel onions.

It was noted that he had worked at the East London Mosque after arriving in the United Kingdom from Bangladesh but had left in 1983 after which he tried to make a living by teaching the Koran in people's homes. After his employment at the East London Mosque was terminated he was still known in the community as the Holy Man. It was noted that he was highly respected in the community and known as a good man.

The police said that they didn't have a motive and did not know why anyone would want to kill him.

The police said that he had had several arguments over debts. He was also noted has having had sent money back to his family in Bangladesh. It was noted that on one occasion a contact of his from Birmingham took the money for him.

It was also noted that he had been selling sarees and trinkets to women throughout the Tower Hamlets area, including times when their husbands were not at home which the police said might have caused some resentment.

On the evening of Tuesday 26 April 1988 at about 9pm he asked the family that he had been living with if he could make a phone call, but he told them that the number he was trying to call was engaged. The family that he had been living with said that they remembered seeing Abdur Rashid looking through a blue book at the time, possibly for a telephone number. However, the book was never found, and the police later said that they thought that the book likely contained the telephone number of Abdur Rashid's murderer and as such a was a vital clue. The family said that when Abdur Rashid finally got through, they overheard the end of his conversation in which he said, 'Alright brothers, I'll come now'.

Abdur Rashid then left the house at about 9.30pm.

He usually attended the East London Mosque for prayers at 10pm, but it appeared that no one saw him there that night.

It was known that Abdur Rashid later visited a friend at a flat in Romford Street at about 11pm at which time he was said to have seemed nervous. He left soon after and was seen shortly after by a friend at about 10.30pm going down a set of stairs in a different block of flats, Block 25, in Romford Street.

He was next seen at about 11.30pm round the corner in Fordham Street by the Sillet Cash and Carry. The person that saw him asked him what he was doing there and said that Abdur Rashid replied, 'I'm waiting, I have something to do'. However, it was not known who he was waiting for or why and no further sightings of him are known.

It was thought that he was murdered sometime later.

It was thought that his murderers might have bought some petrol in a can from a local petrol station, but it was not known where.

After he was murderer his body was taken to Epping Forest. It was thought that his murderers had driven him north along the A11 and had then taken the Epping New Road towards the M25 and then passed the Robin Hood roundabout where they then went left towards High Beach and onto Fairmead Road close to where his body was later found. It was noted the High Beach car park was a popular area for courting couples. It was thought that the car had pulled in about 200 yards along Fairmead road in the early hours and that Abdur Rashid's body was then dumped just inside the wood and set on fire.

It was thought that the flames from the fire would have easily been visible to any passing car. It was also thought that courting couples in the High Beach car park would have been quite likely to have seen the flames and the police urged anyone that saw anything to come forward.

The police later released a picture of the bedspread pattern in the hope that anyone that recognised it might come forward. The police said that they had not otherwise traced the origin of the bedspread. They described it as cream with a green pattern. The police said that they were confident that if they could trace the source of the bedspread that it would lead them to Abdur Rashid's murderer.

At the time Abdur Rashid had a 14-year-old son.

Carol Baldwin

Age: 13

Sex: female

Date: 26 Mar 1988

Place: Lings Wood Park, Northampton, Northamptonshire

Carol Baldwin was stabbed in the back in Lings Wood Park, Northampton on the evening of Saturday 26 March 1988.

She died from internal bleeding after her aorta was punctured by the single stab wound. Her cause of death was given as being due to shock and a massive haemorrhage and nearly two pints of blood were found in her chest cavity.

Her body was found by a group of youths.

A 13-year-old girl was tried for her murder. She had been 12-years-old at the time of the murder and said that she had been elsewhere at the time taking drugs, drinking and having sex. She said that she and a 14-year-old friend had gone off with two 18-year-old boys that they had met earlier in the town centre and had gone to a house in Northampton where they played strip poker and that she then had sex with one of the 18-year-olds. She added that she had sniffed aerosols and had drunk some green liquid that had made her fall over and that she had later watched television and then gone to sleep. She said that they didn't leave the house until 2am the following morning and didn't go to Lings Wood Park.

However, it was said that she had confessed to the murder in a police interview but at her trial said that her confession was untrue. She said that she had become scared after the police refused to believe her repeated denials.

The 13-year-old girl had been in care virtually all her life.

The prosecution said that the 13-year-old girl had attacked Carol Baldwin who was a complete stranger to her after Carol Baldwin had called her a slag. They said that the 13-year-old girl had been sniffing aerosols before the attack. At the girl's trial it was heard that the inhalation of aerosols could have caused decreased awareness and perception.

A knife blade that was later found wedged behind a radiator at a home for girls in council care where the 13-year-old girl had been living was later found and it was said that it could have been the weapon used to have stabbed Carol Baldwin. It was a 4 1/2 inch blade and was found hidden behind the radiator in the children's television room. The handle to the blade was missing, but the police said that forensic scientists who carried out laboratory tests on it had said that when the blade had had a handle that it could have been the one used to kill Carol Baldwin. However, the police noted that without the handle that the blade could easily have caused injury to the hand of the person using it.

However, the 13-year-old girl was cleared by the jury who spent more than seven hours in deliberation.

Shortly after her murder a 17-year-old youth was charged with her murder, but no further action was taken. It was noted that the 17-year-old youth that was charged with Carol Baldwin's murder stood charged at the same time as the 13-year-old girl also stood charged with Carol Baldwin's murder even though there was no known connection between the 17-year-old youth and the 13-year-old girl.

The 17-year-old youth later criticised the police for keeping his clothes following his discharge in mid-May 1988 saying that he had been left with only the clothes that he was standing up in. The police said that releasing his clothes was the responsibility of the Crown Prosecution Services. He had spent nine days in custody. His mother said that the experience had ruined his life.

A 14-year-old girl and a 25-year-old man were also arrested in connection with her murder, but no further action was taken.

Two men were seen wearing uniforms and one of them was traced.

The police said that they were also trying to trace a man in his 60s who regularly walked a golden Labrador dog in the park and two teenage girls who were seen on a nearby footbridge at about the time Carol Baldwin was stabbed.

Carol Baldwin had lived nearby in South Holme Court, Thorplands in Northampton.

She had been walking across a football pitch on her way to a friend's house listening to her father's personal stereo system at the time. It was said that someone had sneaked up behind her and stabbed her. Her father said that he thought that she was catching a bus and said that if he had know that she was walking he would never have let her go.

It was found that Carol Baldwin had kept a secret diary that was found hidden under her pillow which was titled 'Secret Thoughts'. However, the police said that it didn't give them any new leads into her murder. The police said that the diary contained the entries of a typical teenager, going to school, doing homework, going to the dentist, meeting her boyfriend and watching TV. They said that her final entry on 14 March 1988, about a fortnight before she was murdered, was unfinished. The police added that there was nothing in the diary that offered any clues as to who her murderer was.

Following the discovery of her body the police appealed for witnesses, and in particular, anyone that had seen her in Lings Wood Park.

Debbie Linsley

Age: 26

Sex: female

Date: 23 Mar 1988

Place: Victoria Station, London

Debbie Linsley was found dead in a train compartment at Victoria Station on 23 March 1988 at about 2.50pm.

She had been attacked in an old-fashioned train compartment and stabbed at least eleven times to the face, neck and abdomen with at least five stab wounds to the heart. The police said that they thought that she had been attacked with a heavily bladed knife between five and seven-and-a-half inches long. She was found to have defensive injuries indicating that that she had fought back whilst being attacked.

The murder weapon was never found. The police later said that they thought that the knife could be described as a good quality kitchen knife and said that they thought that the murder would have been premeditated as it was unlikely that anyone would have found such a knife in a carriage and that the murderer probably left home with the weapon.

Debbie Linsley was from Bromley but lived and worked in Edinburgh as a hotel receptionist/manager but had come back down to London to attend a hotel management course in Hertfordshire and had taken some additional time off to see some relatives in order to help with preparations for her brothers wedding and to have a bridesmaids dress fitted, which was planned for a few weeks later. She had got on a 2.18pm train from Orpington to Victoria Station in London, boarding at Petts Wood station after being dropped off by her brother there at about 2pm in order to look around the Sherlock Holmes Hotel in Baker Street, London where she had been offered a job by the manager of the hotel after meeting him at the course she had just been on.

There were no more sightings of Debbie Linsley after her brother dropped her off although it was determined that she had bought her train ticket at 2.04pm.

Debbie Linsley had been wearing a blue skirt, white blouse and black leather jacket.

The train had consisted of a mixture of carriages, including come that had common corridors, allowing access from one compartment to another, as well as the older style comparment carriages to which access to the compartments was only possible when the train was at the station. Her mother said however, that Debbie Linsley generally knew the dangers of a closed compartment style carriage and said that when they were tavelling together Debbie Linsley was always mindful of getting into an open style carriage. However, it was noted that Debbie Linsley was a smoker and that the old style carriage was the only carriage that was not a no-smoking carriage and that that was probably why she had got in. The compartment that she had got into was at the front of the second carriage.

It was suggested that when Debbie Linsley had got into the compartment that there might have been other female passengers in it, making her feel safer, but that they might have at some point later got out.

The police said tha they thought that Debbie Linsley had had at least one cigarette whilst in the compartment and that she had also started to eat one of her sandwiches.

They said that there was nothing to indicate that she had been sexually assaulted although added that rape my have been the initial motive of her attacker.

When she was found she still had her belongings with her which ruled out robbery. She had her purse, jewellery and £5 that her brother had just given her.

A passenger in an adjacement compartment, an 18-year-old French au pair, said that she heard screams that lasted for about two minutes coming from the compartment that Debbie Linsley had been in shortly after the train left Brixton railway station. She was later criticised by the coroner at Debbie Linsley's inquest for not pulling the communication cord, but she said that she had been 'glued to her seat' and too shocked to move or pull the communication cord but had contacted the police after she had heard of the murder.

She said, 'I had never heard such screams. They stopped for about five seconds and started again. She called out as if for help. They were screams of fear and very, very loud. I wanted to use the alarm but I remained glued to my seat'.

She later followed a man that got out of the last compartment of the first carriage and a photofit was released of him, but he was never traced.

The train had stopped at Bickley, Bromley South, Shortlands, Beckenham Juction, Kent House, Penge East, Sydenham Hill, West Dulwich, Herne Hill and Brixton. The joureny would have taken only 31 minutes.

Relevant train times are:

- **Petts Wood**: 2.18pm.
- **Penge East**: (five stops from Victoria) 2.34pm. Here a man was seen by a woman hurredly changing compartments on the train and is was thought that he might have got into Debbie Linsley's compartment and might have been the murderer.
- **Brixton**: 2.43pm. French au pair hears screaming.
- **Victoria**: 2.49pm. French au pair said that when she got out at Victoria she saw a man with red hair getting out of the compartment next to the one that Debbie Linsley had been in. She said that she followed the man out of the

platform but lost sight of him in the
concourse.
- **Victoria**: 2.50pm. Debbie Linsley's
  body was found by a porter who was
  checking each compartment and
  carriage.

It was thought that there had been about 70
passengers that had used the train but only
the French au pair had heard anything
although some later reported having heard a
commotion but didn't investigate. The ticket
collectors at the platform said that between
30 to 40 people got off the train at Victoria
but the police said that only 26 of them had
been accounted for. The police added that
they thought that there would have been at
least 20 other people that had been on the
train that had not as yet come forward.

The Daily Mirror published a set of times
that the train would have arrived at each of
the stations in its newspaper on Friday 25
March 1988, stating that the train would stop
for no more than 20 to 30 seconds at each
stop:

- **Depart Orpington**: 2.16pm.
- **Petts Wood**: 2.18pm.
- **Bickley**: 2.22pm.
- **Bromley South**: 2.25pm.
- **Shortlands**: 2.27pm.

- **Beckenham Junction**: 2.30pm.
- **Kent House**: 2.32pm.
- **Penge East**: 2.34pm.
- **Sydenham Hill**: 2.37pm.
- **West Dulwich**: 2.41pm.
- **Herne Hill**: 2.41pm.
- **Brixton**: 2.43pm.
- **Victoria**: 2.51pm.

The newspaper noted that the longest time between stations was eight minutes between Brixton and Victoria and that her murderer might have killed her in the half-mile-long tunnel between Penge East and Sydenham Hill.

When the police searched the compartment they found that Debbie Linsley had injured her attacker whose blood it was thought was found there. It was also noted that a man was seen walking away from platform two with blood and an injury on his face which was thought might have been caused by Debbie Linsley as she defended herself. However, the police have not as yet been able to match the DNA from the blood samples with anyone. The police said that they were still hopeful that they could trace the man's DNA through familial DNA searches.

During their investigation the police took over 1,200 statements and ruled out over 650 potential suspects.

The police released details of several people that they were trying to trace:

- A short stocky man that was seen jumping from the train at Victoria.
- The man that the French au pair saw getting out of the last compartment of the first carriage (Debbie Linsley had been in the first compartment of the second carriage). He was described as being aged about 40, well built, muscular rather than fat, reddish brown hair and with a moustache with that followed the contour of his lips, and wearing a light wind cheater and grey trousers. A photofit was released of him.
- A man was seen walking away from platform two at Victoria with blood and a cut on his face about ten minutes after the train pulled in. A man was seen a while later in the gentlemans toilets at Victoria station cleaning a cut on his head. It was thought that he was not the same person that the French au pair had seen getting off the train. He was described as being in his late 20s, 5ft 5in tall, with long ash-blond hair and with scratches on his left cheek. However, the police noted that there had been a

football match on and that there had been several fights and that he could well have been involved in those and not Debbie Linsley's murder.

- A man was seen leaving one of the compartment on the train at Penge East and to then get back on board, possibly into the compartment that Debbie Linsley had been in. He was described as being aged about 30 years, with a stocky build, dirty blond hair, a scruffy appearance and wearing a pale brown jacket.
- A man was seen staring at women getting on the train at Orpington.

The police said that it was possible that the attack had started off as an attempted rape although they said that there was no evidence of any sexual attack about her body.

It was noted that Debbie Linsley had been security conscious and used to carry a rape whistle with her on her keyring.

The police also said that they thought that Debbie Linsley was not her killers first victim and that he had probably attacked women before. It was said that the ferosity of the injuries indicated that her attacker had attacked other people. A detective on the case said that he thought that it was puzzling that whilst they had the murderers DNA and that he was probably a repeat violent offender, that they had not been able to trace him.

Debbie Linsley had had a boyfriend in Scotland.

Severed Limbs

Age: 25 to 35

Sex: female

Date: 12 Mar 1988

Place: Sturry Street, East India Dock Road, A13, Docklands, East London

The severed limbs of her woman were found in East London on the morning of Saturday 12 March 1988.

Her identity was unknown although the woman was described as being a white adult aged in her late 20s or early 30s. The police said that due to the size of the limbs that they thought that she had been a fairly well built woman and at least ten or eleven stone in weight, of medium build. They also estimated her height to be about 5ft 7in, give or take an inch either way.

She had been dead for between 24 and 48 hours. The remains were found off the East India Dock Road, A13 near a women's refuge in Sturry Street. The remains were left buy some bins at the refuge wrapped up in black plastic packages. It was thought that the packages had been left there sometime between 6.30pm on the Friday 11 March 1988 and 10am Saturday 13 March 1988. The dustbins were up the stairs at the refuge off the street. The packages were said to have been neatly wrapped.

The packages contained two arms and two legs.

The nails of the hands were found to have been bitten right back which it was said suggested that the woman had lived on her nerves and was very nervous and had chewed them.

Red nail varnish was found on her big toe. There was no sign of nail polish on her fingers.

It was also noted that her left leg was slightly longer than the right, but the police said that that would not have produced a noticeable limp.

It was noted that there was some scaring on her left wrist, which the home office pathologist said suggested that she had previously attempted suicide. It was also noted that she had a small fracture to her ankle in one of her long bones suggesting that she might have fallen sometime before her death, but it was noted that she might not have noticed. The home office pathologist said that the limbs suggested that she had been very active and that she might have done a lot of dancing. The pathologist also said that they thought that she had also frequently wore high heels due to the crowding of her toes. It was also noted that she had a joining of two toes on both feet which was described as a congenital abnormality. It was said that her joining toes, whilst not giving her a lot of trouble, would have been quite noticeable.

The police said that an indentation on the middle finger of her right hand indicated that she had worn a ring there.

Her blood group was found to be Group B, which they said was a fairly unusual group.

The Home Office pathologist said that when they checked the libs for drugs, they found traces of benzodiazepine which indicated that she had taken tranquilisers such as Valium or Librium.

The police said that after considering the evidence that they thought that she might have at some time suffered from depression and once been suicidal.

It was also noted that a man was seen sitting in a dark blue Cortina car parked just off the East India Dock Road near the refuge at about 9.30pm on Friday 11 March 1988, the night before the packages were found. The man that was seen sitting in the car had been wearing glasses and smoking a cigarette and was described as being of Mediterranean appearance.

Michel Becouarn

Age: 43

Sex: male

Date: 22 Feb 1988

Place: Kingsmead Estate, Malvern Road, Hackney

Michel Becouarn was stabbed to death with his own samurai sword.

His 24-year-old son was tried for his murder at the Old Bailey but was found not guilty.

It was claimed that his son had killed him with the sword during a drunken argument. They had been out drinking together during the day, but Michel Becouarn's son said that he had been out walking the dog when the attack took place after they had a row and Michel Becouarn kicked him out.

It was said that the police had been informed of the murder by an anonymous phone call to them, but it was determined that it had been Michel Becouarn's son that had made the call. Michel Becouarn's son said that he had found his father dead on the bedroom floor when he got back and thought that he would get into trouble and so went out and made the call to the police, pretending to be a neighbour.

However, Michel Becouarn's son was arrested when he returned home.

Michel Becouarn had been attacked from behind with the sword.

The sword was an ornamental samurai sword and it was said that one of the blows had been made with such force that it had gone right through his back and out through his chest.

Michel Becouarn had kept the sword for his own protection.

Following the son's acquittal, the police said that there were no other lines of enquiry and as far as they were concerned the case was closed unless any further information came to light.

Michel Becouarn and his son had both been street traders.

John Lennon

Age: 41

Sex: male

Date: 20 Feb 1988

Place: Anthonys Road, Forest Gate, East London

John Lennon was found dead in Anthonys Road, Forest Gate, East London in the early hours of 20 February 1988.

His pockets were turned out and he had been robbed.

He had a small bruise to his neck and his post mortem stated that his cause of death was massive bleeding into his brain from a torn neck artery.

He was described as an Irish drunk and had been a paint sprayer. He was of no fixed address but had lived in the Plumstead and North Woolwich areas.

He had spent his last night with his girlfriend drinking in the Upton Manor public house in Plashet Road, Plaistow and it was heard that she was the last person other than his murderer or murderers to see him alive.

A man was tried for his murder but acquitted. He said that he had been at home asleep in front of his television at the time. He was arrested five months after John Lennon was found dead.

He said that at the time his aunt from Jamaica had been over to London for a visit and that it was her last night and so he had stayed in to see her.

When he was arrested five months after John Lennon's murder he was quoted as having said, 'Why me? What have I done?'. However, it was said that he had confessed to some other prisoners whilst on remand at Bristol police station. It was said that he had demonstrated how he had killed John Lennon and that he had boasted about it. However, the man denied murdering John Lennon and was acquitted of both murder and manslaughter.

John Lawrence

Age: unknown

Sex: male

Date: 7 Feb 1988

Place: Isleworth

John Lawrence was murdered in his flat in Percy Road, Isleworth.

He was murdered sometime between 4.40pm on Sunday 7 February 1988 and 10am on Tuesday 9 February 1988.

He had lived in a flat at the back of a house at the corner of Percy Road and Worple Road in Isleworth.

Several items were stolen from his flat including a Nesco compact disc player.

A neighbour said that they heard a distressed cry from his flat between 10.30pm and midnight on Sunday 7 February 1988 and the police said that they were looking to trace two youths that had been seen outside of his flat at about the same time. It was said that although it was cold, one of the youths was seen to take off a dark speckly pullover, revealing a light-coloured t-shirt. It was also said that he had seemed upset and that the other youth had appeared to be consoling him.

John Lawrence was an ophthalmic nursing tutor and also a homosexual and it was said that he frequently visited pubs and casinos where he met young men.

It was noted that although he had eaten a large lunch on the Sunday, a frying pan was found in the kitchen with a hamburger and chips in it and the table was laid for one with a choice of sauces and it was suggested that he had been cooking for someone else.

On Monday 8 February 1988 his wallet, jewellery, letters and credit cards were found at Twickenham railway station on waste ground below stairs leading to the Waterloo platform. The police appealed for anyone that had been waiting at Twickenham station for the 1.22am train for Waterloo in the early hours of Monday 8 February 1988 that saw anything to come forward.

However, his red Royal College of Nursing diary and his watch were never found.

Graeme Stack

Age: 23

Sex: male

Date: 1 Feb 1988

Place: Deptford High Street, London

Graeme Stack was stabbed in the street late at night.

A sociology student was tried for his manslaughter but acquitted.

Graeme Stack was last seen chasing a man whilst drunk and trying to get his trilby hat.

He was next seen staggering about with a wound and then fell hitting his head causing brain damage from which he later died.

Graeme Stack was unemployed and had lived in Eltham.

It was said that in the early hours of Saturday 27 January 1988 that he had chased the sociology student down Deptford

High Street shouting, 'Oi wanker, give me your hat'.

It was said that Graeme Stack was a heavy drinker and had been four times over the drink drive limit.

Some young men that had been waiting for a mini-cab saw Graeme Stack chasing the sociology student and then go out of sight. However, they said that when Graeme Stack reappeared, he appeared to be staggering and to be covered in blood. They said that he got as far as a building site and then fell backwards and cracked his head.

He was taken to hospital by a passing ambulance where it was found that he had been stabbed in the abdomen resulting in his liver being lacerated. He was operated on immediately and whilst still in intensive care he was later taken back to the operating theatre where surgeons carried out an operation on his brain which had been injured by the fall. However, he died a few days later.

His cause of death was given as being due to his head injury, but it was noted that that was consequent on having been stabbed in the abdomen shortly before.

The sociology student, who admitted to having been carrying a Swiss Army knife on him at the time for defence denied stabbing Graeme Stack. He said that Graeme Stack had chased him two thirds of his way home to his student halls of residence in Creek Street, Deptford and said that when he got back, he told his friends what had happened. He said that later that day he went home to his parent's house in Reading.

The sociology student, who was studying at Goldsmith's College, was later questioned by the police and after his second interview he was charged with Graeme Stack's manslaughter.

He was tried at the Old Bailey but acquitted on Monday 15 February 1988.

Ian Bushell

Age: 21

Sex: male

Date: 20 Jan 1988

Place: Thamesmead, London

Ian Bushell went missing on 20 January 1988.

When his flat was entered on 16 February 1988 all his possessions were still there including his clothes, wallet and keys.

Nothing more is known about his disappearance.

Yana Jones

Age: 28

Sex: female

Date: 16 Jan 1988

Place: Rutley Close, Walworth

Yana Jones was found dead in her flat on Rutley Close, Walworth on 16 January 1988.

She had been stabbed three times in the neck and face. She was found by a friend lying in a pool of blood.

Her inquest heard that there were no signs of there having been a forced entry into her flat or that she had attempted to defend herself with it was said indicated that she had known her murderer and that she had invited him in.

It was thought that up to £300 had been stolen by her murderer or murderers.

The police said that they had followed many leads and interviewed a number of people in connection with her murder but said that it appeared that people appeared unwilling to help them.

Anthony Gardner

Age: 26

Sex: male

Date: 9 Jan 1988

Place: Gretney Walk, Moss Side, Manchester

Anthony Gardner was shot at point blank range with a sawn off-shotgun as he sat in a car in Moss Side.

Anthony Gardner had been in the front passenger seat.

It was thought that his murder was a gangland hit after he fell out with a gang leader.

A man, Anthony Johnson, was suspected of his murder but was himself later murdered in 1991, which is also unsolved.

Shortly after the shooting, the police said that it was 'a premeditated and deliberate shooting. They also added, 'We have no idea about the motive for this murder'.

It was said that the car that Anthony Gardner had been in had pulled up in Gretney Walk, Moss Side outside a sheban and that a gunman had stepped out from the shadows and shot Anthony Gardner through the windscreen as he sat in the passenger seat.

It was said that after the shooting that the people in the sheban fled before the police arrived and threw their drugs away in the street resulting in the police finding over £1,000 worth of heroin and cocaine lying about.

Anthony Gardner was also known as Scratch.

Printed in Great Britain
by Amazon